SS CSE ENGLISH

A Practical Approach to
WRITING SKILLS

Duncan Beal ◆ David Stone

First published in 2003 by:
Nelson Thornes Ltd
Delta Place
27 Bath Road
CHELTENHAM
GL53 7TH
United Kingdom

03 04 05 06 07 / 10 9 8 7 6 5 4 3 2 1

A catalogue record for this book is available from the British Library

ISBN 0 7487 7464 5

Developed and produced by Start to Finish

Typeset by Paul Manning
Printed and bound in Italy by Canale

Contents

Introduction

The National Curriculum states that you should learn to write for certain specific purposes during your time in secondary school, at Key Stage 3 and Key Stage 4. These purposes are examined by all of the examination boards at GCSE. The purposes are collected together in four clusters of three. These are known, by your teachers and by examiners, as 'the writing triplets'. The four clusters are:

- Writing to imagine, explore, entertain
- Writing to argue, persuade, advise
- Writing to inform, explain, describe
- Writing to analyse, review, comment.

You are probably familiar with the skills and practice required for the first of these – writing to imagine, explore, entertain – since it most readily produces narrative writing. The other three triplets require particular skills and practice. You may have to respond to them either as a coursework assignment or in answer to an examination question, depending upon which examination board you are entered with. This book takes you through the skills and practice you will need for the three clusters:

- Writing to argue, persuade, advise
- Writing to inform, explain, describe
- Writing to analyse, review, comment.

Many examiners would agree with the view that students spend most of their preparation and revision time for English focusing on the Reading requirements of the syllabus. Many senior examiners would also hold the view that, for many students, their responses to Reading assignments and questions are better than their responses to Writing. The purpose of this book is to help you improve your understanding of what is required in Writing for GCSE, show you examples of successful writing, explain the skills and methods you need to adopt to write successfully yourself and give you lots of practice activities. Remember, there is exactly the same number of marks available for the Writing part of your English GCSE as there is for the Reading part.

This book contains twelve units of work for each of the three writing triplets. The pattern of each unit is the same. You analyse and explore some modelled writing through a series of comments, hints, information and activities, after which there is a major unit activity, with guidance, so that you can practise the skills learned from the modelled writing.

You will be able to submit, as coursework assignments, the best of the tasks you undertake from the book. You will also have had lots of practice for the triplets which will appear in your examination papers.

Improving your writing skills, in a way which is focused on the GCSE triplets, is probably the most advantageous thing you could do to improve your English grade.

This book will do that for you.

Unit 1.1

Writing to argue

The unit activity is to write a speech for a debate (see page 9).

LOOKING FOR AN ARGUMENT

M = *man looking for an argument*
A = *arguer (John Cleese)*

Outside 12a. The man knocks on the door.

A: (*from within*) Come in.
The man enters the room. The arguer is sitting at a desk.

M: Is this the right room for an argument?

A: I've told you *once*.

M: No you haven't.

A: Yes I have.

M: When?

A: Just now!

M: No you didn't.

A: Yes I did!

M: Didn't.

A: Did.

M: Didn't.

A: I'm telling you I did!

M: You did not!

A: I'm sorry, is this a five-minute argument, or the full half-hour?

M: Oh ... Just a five-minute one.

A: Fine (*makes a note of it; the man sits down*) thank you. Anyway, I did.

M: You most certainly did not.

A: Now, let's get one thing *quite* clear. I most definitely told you!

M: You did not.

A: Yes I did.

M: You did not.

A: Yes I did.

M: Didn't.

A: Yes I did.

M: Didn't.

A: Yes I did!!

M: Look this isn't an argument.

A: Yes it is.

M: No it isn't, it's just contradiction.

A: No it isn't.

M: Yes it is.

A: It is not.

M: It is. You just contradicted me.

A: No I didn't.

M: Ooh you did!

A: No, no, no, no, no.

M: You did, just then.

A: No, nonsense!

M: Oh, look this is futile.

A: No it isn't.

M: I came here for a good argument.

A: No you didn't, you came here for an *argument*.

M: Well an argument's not the same as contradiction.

A: It can be.

M: No it can't. An argument is a connected series of statements to establish a definite proposition.

A: No it isn't.

M: Yes it is. It isn't just contradiction.

A: Look, if I argue with you I must take up a contrary position.

M: But it isn't just saying 'No it isn't.'

A: Yes it is.

M: No it isn't, argument is an intellectual process ... contradiction is just the automatic gainsaying of anything the other person says.

A: No it isn't.

M: Yes it is.

A: Not at all.

M: Now look!

A: (*pressing the bell on his desk*) Thank you, good morning.

M: What?

A: That's it. Good morning.

M: But I was just getting interested.

A: Sorry the five minutes is up.

from the Argument Clinic sketch in Monty Python's Flying Circus: Just the Words

Making a start

A	Most people like a good argument.
B	No they don't.
A	Yes they do. In an argument you can explore ideas, test your reasoning powers …
B	No, you're missing the point. It's competitive. You have a winner. You get one over other people. You can try out different insults; you can really wind people up …
A	Stop! That's not an *argument*; that's a *row*. An argument is not about personal abuse. It's about developing a point of view, not simply contradicting what others say.

So what does **to argue** mean if it does not mean to row? Here are some dictionary definitions:

- to discuss with reasoning
- to persuade by reasoning into or out of an opinion or a course of action
- to give reason to believe.

The words *reason* or *reasoning* occur in all three definitions.

An **argument** consists of a step-by-step progression of reasons, each one a small argument in itself. Taken together, they contribute towards the overall effectiveness of the argument.

- The **aim** of an argument is to influence someone to your point of view.
- The **subject** of an argument is an issue about which people disagree. It always assumes that other reasonable people can have opposing but equally valid points of view.
- The **audience** or readership of an argument is those people you wish to convince or sway to your point of view. The methods you choose to present your argument should take into account the type of audience you are addressing.

Activity 1.1a Read the comedy sketch opposite.

1 Which lines do you think help to define what an argument is?
2 Which lines are no more than rowing or abuse?

What sort of argument might you be asked to write?

Often you will be given a statement and invited to write *for* or *against* it.

- The statement may be a moral question about the way we live our lives, for example, 'Lying is always wrong'.
- It may be a controversial issue, such as the rights and wrongs of fox hunting, or of giving foreign aid to poorer countries.
- It may be a matter of personal opinion on a more personal or local issue, such as the advantages of being an only child, or whether local facilities are adequate.

Often you will also be given:

- a **form**, for example, the form may be a speech, a feature article or a letter to a local newspaper
- an **audience**, for example, this may be your class, the headteacher, local councillors or the readers of a newspaper.

Activity 1.1b

1 Choose one of these statements:
- ● The school day should be longer.
- ● Homework is unnecessary.
- ● All teenagers should do voluntary work in the community.
- ● Parenting should be a compulsory subject in school.

Working in pairs, one of you should argue *for* or *against* the chosen statement for no more than a minute. Your partner should then try to counter your arguments.

2 Choose another statement and swap roles.

What did you find were the problems in developing a convincing argument? Was your argument 'a connected series of statements', or did you simply contradict each other? You probably found that it is very difficult to assemble an effective argument without proper preparation and notes.

An argument

Read this argument written in response to Unit Activity 1.1:

KEY WORDS

To argue effectively you will need to develop a vocabulary of useful words and phrases. Look at the words below.

Some words from the Monty Python sketch:

to contradict
To deny what someone else has said.

a proposition
A statement with which people may agree or disagree. Many written arguments begin with a proposition.

Some important opposites:
logical/illogical
valid argument/false argument
convincing/unconvincing
fact/opinion
rational/irrational
rational/emotive
propose/oppose

Test each other on the spelling of the words above and these too:
argue/argued/arguing/argument
disagree/disagreed/disagreeing
persuade/persuasion/persuasive

'It's always wrong to lie.'
Write a speech for a school debate for or against this statement.

I disagree with the statement. There are occasions in life when lying is not only acceptable, but actually better than the truth.

When my mum returned from the hairdresser's last week and asked for my opinion of the result, I could tell from the look on her face that only one answer was expected, and I gave it. It was not the truth, but it was tactful. I was not entirely truthful to save my mum's feelings.

What was my motive in lying? Was it to deceive and gain advantage for myself? No. My intention was actually quite noble. And here is an important distinction: between lying in order to harm and cause mischief, and lying in order to 'keep the peace'.

So it is the word 'always' in the statement that I disagree with. If you lie in a court of law and the wrong person is convicted; if you spread malicious, untrue

---

gossip about people; if you lie about your behaviour to people close to you: then lying is wrong. But *always*? What about the white lies we tell to avoid bad feeling? What about those who go undercover to expose fraud and crime? What about all the little lies of social etiquette: 'Nice to see you; Do drop in anytime'? In fact a world where everyone told the truth all the time might not be very pleasant.

An intentional attempt to deceive for your own gain is wrong, but life is too complex to say that all lying is always wrong. Ladies and gentlemen, I ask you to consider how many lies you have told today before voting on this proposal.

Activity 1.1c
1 What is the proposition for the argument?
2 What is the form?
3 Who is the audience?
4 How does this written argument differ from the argument in the Monty Python sketch?

Having identified the purpose, form and audience of the speech, you can analyse the **techniques of persuasion** used, and how the writer keeps in mind the form and the audience.

Activity 1.1d Find evidence in the speech of the following features:
- an awareness of the audience
- a clearly stated point of view
- a planned progression of paragraphs
- an awareness of the form of writing – that this is a speech
- an awareness of the key words in the statement or proposition
- a logical, step-by-step development

- use of specific techniques of persuasion:
  – anecdote (a story or example from real life)
  – questions to provoke thought
  – variety in sentence length
  – a recognition of the opposing point of view
  – a sincere, calm tone
  – a punchy, challenging conclusion.

> **WHAT EXAMINERS ARE LOOKING FOR**
> The grade C description for a task such as Unit Activity 1.1 is:
> 'The style and tone convey meaning and intention clearly, adapting these to the specified purpose and audience.'
> In other words, remember that this is a **speech** for a **class debate**!

Serious practice

UNIT ACTIVITY 1.1 'It's always wrong to lie.'
Write a speech for a school debate for or against this statement.

The speech on page 8 was written *against* this statement. You are speaking in the same debate, but for the opposing point of view.

With a partner, first discuss some arguments you could use to *support* the proposition that it is always wrong to lie.

Write your speech countering some of the arguments used in the speech on page 8. Try to use some of the techniques identified in this unit.

> **Hint**
> Read the question carefully. Identify the words which refer to the purpose, form and audience.

WHERE DO I GET IDEAS FOR AN ARGUMENT?
Discussion with others always helps to generate ideas, but that is not possible in an examination.

In the exam, spend a few minutes brainstorming the topic, then use numbers to arrange your ideas into paragraphs. For example, you could note the following points in response to the speech on page 8:

1 Better to be brutally frank than trying to please people all the time.
2 Lying may save people's feelings – that doesn't make it 'right'.
3 We are not arguing about how we actually behave, but on the proposition: it is always wrong to lie.
4 Lying in small things ('white lies') can lead to lying in important ways. It becomes a habit.

A better order for these ideas might be: 2, 1, 4, 3.

Always try to include some **personal experience** (anecdote). If you cannot think of an appropriate story from life to illustrate your point, you could always make one up. But would that be a problem when you are arguing that it is always wrong to lie ...?

Unit 1.2

Writing to persuade

The unit activity is to write a persuasive letter to a newspaper (see page 13).

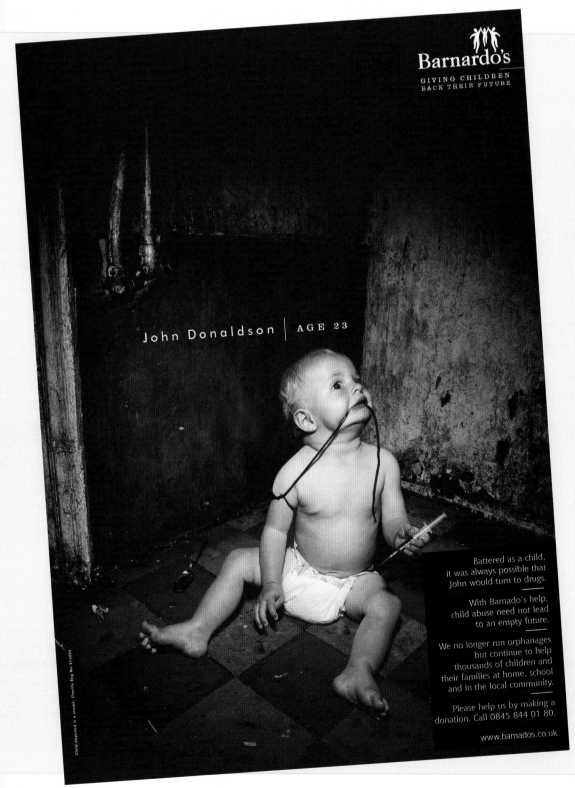

'We would love to be able to use soft cuddly images all the time, but we feel we must raise public awareness of the deprivation that can blight the lives of thousands of children today.'

Is this advert too sick?

from The Express, 21 January 2000

'Adverts need to be more subtle.'

'Anything that brings attention to drug abuse and opens the debate is to be welcomed.'

'Basically the advert is saying, "Here's an awful picture – send us some money". I feel Barnardo's has dishonoured the good name it got from running orphanages.'

Committee of Advertising Practice explaining why they were urging newspapers not to publish the advertisement:

Too shocking … Shocking adverts risk alienating the very people they want to reach …. People should think twice before accepting this ad. Children are one of the most sensitive subjects, and so are drugs.

Making a start

The **purpose** of the advertisement opposite is to persuade us to donate to the charity Barnardo's. But how did people react to this advertisement when it appeared? Some responses are shown above.

Techniques of persuasion

What techniques have the advertisers used to persuade readers to donate to the charity?

Activity 1.2a	1	Work in a pair or small group to discuss your own reaction to this advertisement.
	2	Read the extract below about the making of the advertisement. Does knowing this affect your view?

The advertisers say the filth, needle and syringe were added after the 15-month-old baby was photographed and the parents and Barnardo's staff were present throughout the shoot.
　　The site was cleaned and disinfected, a clear film added over the floor surface to protect the child and the baby's contorted expression added by computer post-production.

from The Express, 21 January 2000

Hints

These questions will help you decide on your response for question 1 of Activity 1.2a:

1 How is **contrast** used in the words and the images? (Example: the vulnerable baby in squalid surroundings.)

2 How is the **layout** of the advertisement designed for maximum impact? (Look at the arrangement of words and images; the composition; how your eye moves over the advertisement.)

3 Do you have any concerns about the making of this advertisement?

4 What is your response to it? Does the advertisement make you think, or is your response more emotional?

5 Does this advertisement pass the test: does it persuade you to give money to Barnardo's?

Is there any difference between argument and persuasion?

Argument and **persuasion** are closely linked. All argument writing is about persuading or influencing the reader to your point of view.

Unit 1.1 showed that argument involves using reason to present a point of view. This includes a cool consideration of opposing points of view.

Persuasion is more personal and single-minded. It seeks to change other people's ideas or behaviour. It tends to appeal to our emotions more openly, and it does not usually consider the other point of view.

The Barnardo's advertisement is a way of persuading which uses both **emotional appea**l (our concern for a vulnerable baby) and **rational argument** (making us think about the link between the innocent child of the advertisement and the adult he will become).

Activity 1.2b

Look at the arguments presented by the words and visual images in the advertisement. Put the following statements into a logical order so that a clear argument appears.

1   It is possible to help people who are abused in childhood to a happy adulthood.
2   Send a donation to Barnardo's.
3   Everyone is born innocent.
4   We cannot help personally, but if we are moved to pity our money can make a difference.
5   Childhood experiences can destroy happiness in later life.
6   Some people are likely to turn to drugs because of unhappy childhoods.
7   Barnardo's has the expertise to help abused children overcome early experiences.

HEAD OR HEART?

Your head is supposed to be the source of rational thinking, and your heart is traditionally where feelings come from. If one person is said to be 'ruled by his head' and another to be 'ruled by his heart', what sort of people are they?

Units 1.1 and 1.2 show that to be persuasive we need to make an appeal to both head *and* heart, to the mind as well as to the emotions.

Some 'head' words:

reason
A support, a justification, a cause, for holding a point of view (*Give me two reasons …*, *It stands to reason*).

reasoning
Using logical thought (*use reasoning to solve that problem*).

rational
Using reason; intelligent (*She took a rational decision*).

Some 'heart' words:

emotional
Concerned with feelings rather than thoughts.

emotional appeal
Invites us to feel sympathy for someone, or makes us feel angry about an injustice. We have an **emotional response**.

emotive language
Language which appeals to our feelings. *Defenceless pensioner brutally mugged for Christmas savings* in a newspaper headline is more likely to arouse our pity than *Seventy-two-year-old woman robbed*. The first headline uses words with an emotional appeal. This is emotive language.

Serious practice

Too shocking?

Several newspapers and magazines decided not to carry the Barnardo's advertisement because it was too shocking and upsetting for readers. Some people felt that the advertisement was simply out to shock, and that instead of increasing donations, it would have the opposite effect.

UNIT ACTIVITY 1.2 Your local newspaper decides at the last minute not to run the advertisement. Its argument is that young children might well look at the paper and be upset. They would take in only the visual image, not the words, and would therefore not understand the message.

Write a letter to your local newspaper either supporting their decision or arguing that the advertisement should be printed.

WHAT EXAMINERS ARE LOOKING FOR

Mark schemes for letters in GCSE examinations state that a successful answer will 'create an appropriate register for a letter'.

Register means the type of language you use in certain situations. How formal do you need to be? What level of knowledge and understanding do you expect your readers to have?

Hints

- First, read the question carefully. Identify the words which refer to the purpose, form and audience.
- Jot down the arguments you would like to use. Consider the various views presented in this unit, and ideas from other people in the class.
- **First draft** Having assembled your arguments, put them in a logical order, and try to group them into three or four paragraphs, each with a clear topic.

- **Edit** Now consider persuasive techniques. How will you begin in order to grab your reader's attention? How will you finish? Is it appropriate to include an emotional appeal, or would you rather stick to rational argument?
- **Proof-read** Check for accuracy of spelling and punctuation. Are there some words from the first two units which you could use? Is each paragraph a collection of sentences on a topic? Have you avoided one-sentence paragraphs?

LETTER-WRITING

If you are asked to write a letter in an examination you do not need to include addresses unless you are asked to.

One reason why the setting out of a letter is not examined is because there is no clear agreement about the correct way of starting or ending a letter. The 'rules' about setting out letters change according to where you are in the English-speaking world, and according to which textbook you read.

Take a look at this recommended website: www.plainenglish.com. The site is devoted to providing clear guidance on such things as the modern way of presenting addresses (no punctuation required) as well as useful advice on aspects of written English, such as how to write a report or a CV.

Most letters to national or local newspapers start with *Sir*. You might consider that to be outdated in the modern age, in which case *Dear Sir/Madam* would be quite acceptable.

The ending is generally *Yours sincerely* or *Yours faithfully*, then the first name and surname of the writer.

See Units 1.4 and 1.6 for further advice and practice in letter-writing.

Unit 1.3

Writing to advise

The unit activity is to write a report giving advice (see page 17).

Extract A

My son, 11, isn't coping with secondary school. He's had detention, constantly loses kit and doesn't seem able to master any subject. He hates it and is very unhappy. He seems so much younger than his peers. Would home tuition help or would this make him very isolated? Do I have other options?

IF YOU ASK ME ...

Advice 1: A headteacher:
… It is essential that this boy remains in full-time education. Home tuition is certainly not the answer. The longer he stayed out of the classroom the harder it would become for him to integrate back into school. It's early in the school year, and young children are highly adaptable and usually able to settle into new environments. This boy may be sensitive, possibly a late developer, perhaps taking more time than his contemporaries to come to terms with his new school. As he is having difficulties with his possessions it would be worth investing five minutes each morning helping him to plan his day and organise his books and kit …

Advice 2: A headteacher:
Parents and teachers should first be aware that school does not suit all, and that some children need a different environment, which may be home schooling or a small school … Did the child show signs of stress at primary school, especially at times of transition, but cope eventually? If the answer is yes, then it is likely he will also adjust here. Secondary schools should have a head of year or form tutor to address the difficulties facing children at the start of Year 7 …

Advice 3: Representative from Human Scale Education:
Unhappy children can't learn. First, I would discover what the school suggests. Ultimately it's the school's responsibility to meet a child's needs, and this one seems to be failing. In a large school, your son's problems may pass unnoticed. Or you could look at alternative schools in the area. Your son might be happier in a smaller establishment. Home education is also an option and doesn't have to be isolating: you can do it with other parents. Thousands of parents, many with no teaching experience, home educate very successfully.

from Guardian Education, 10 December 2002

Making a start

Writing to **advise** belongs with writing to **argue** and **persuade** because all three types of writing involve influencing people's thoughts and behaviour.

Writing to advise deals with real or imaginary problems and offers practical solutions. The intended reader of your advice might be a friend facing a personal difficulty, or an organisation seeking guidance on a future course of action. These are some typical 'writing to advise' questions you are likely to come across:

- *A friend has an opportunity to study abroad for a year. Write advising him or her whether to take up the offer.*
- *A friend needs advice on whether to go to college or take up a full-time job and earn some money for a car.*
- *A friend who has had difficulties with parents over personal freedom is thinking of leaving home. Write to him or her with advice.*
- *Your headteacher is considering changing the school uniform. Write a report advising on what should be done.*
- *The local council want advice on how to improve youth facilities. Write a letter with your ideas.*
- *Write a leaflet for newcomers to your area advising on how they might make the most of local facilities and avoid pitfalls.*

As you can see, you will need to be able to write in a variety of **forms**, for example, letter, report, leaflet.

KEY WORDS
Learn the different forms of the key word in writing to advise:

advise

The verb form – the final sound is *z*. For example: *I have to advise you that …*; *I was advised not to …*; *Advising people can be dangerous.*

advice

The noun form – the final sound is *s* rather than *z*. For example: *That was sound advice*; *My advice is …*; *I decided against their advice.*

adviser/advisor

A person who gives advice – both spellings are correct.

Activity 1.3a Read the letter from a worried parent and the advice offered in Extract A. What do you think about the advice offered?

1   Write down any phrases which you think help to identify the problem or to offer sound advice. Some phrases have been underlined in Advice 2 as an example.
2   Compare your chosen phrases with those of a partner.
3   Discuss:
   a) Which adviser do you think addresses the problem most sensibly? Why?
   b) The parent asks whether there are 'other options'. Do you think that there are other useful pieces of advice not mentioned by the three writers?

Techniques in writing to advise

The advisers in Extract A use the following techniques in their writing.

- **Use of the personal pronouns *I* and *you*.** This technique can give a warm, sympathetic tone to the advice (see Advice 3).
- **Strong statements of opinion.** Two of the advisers state opinions very strongly as if they were accepted facts. This technique gives the views force and conviction.
- **Varied sentence length.** Short sentences, when surrounded by longer sentences, help to emphasise the views expressed within them.
- **Use of questions.** One of the advisers uses a question to highlight how limited the information given is, and therefore how difficult it is to give advice.

Hint

Suggested paragraph plan for Activity 1.3b:

- **Paragraph 1: Identify the problem**
  Look at the child's behaviour and attitude, and try to sum up the nature of the problem as you see it.
- **Paragraph 2: Consider the options**
  Home tuition? Change schools? Address the problem within the school? Do nothing?
- **Paragraph 3: Your advice**

Activity 1.3b

1 Look again at the advice given in Extract A. Find examples of the techniques listed on page 15.
2 Write your own advice to the parent, using your ideas from Activity 1.3a. Try to include some of the techniques and useful words and phrases for this type of writing shown on this page.
  Your advice should be about one side of writing.

USEFUL WORDS AND PHRASES

Some words and phrases are frequently used in advisory and persuasive writing to guide the reader through the ideas and views expressed. They are often known as **signpost words** (the technical term is **discourse markers**).

Ways of starting paragraphs or sentences:

Firstly, …
Suggests an ordered sequence of ideas to follow.

However, …
Means *on the other hand …, in contrast …*.
It signals that the advice or argument is about to present another point of view, going off in a new direction.

Ways of bringing the writing to a conclusion:

Finally, …
In conclusion, …
Therefore, ….

When used in this way, all these adverbs should be separated from the rest of the sentence by a comma

Expert advice

Extract B is a short piece of advice from a student health leaflet.

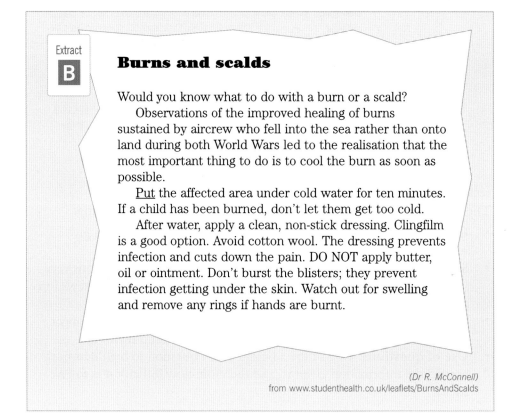

Extract **B**

Burns and scalds

Would you know what to do with a burn or a scald?

Observations of the improved healing of burns sustained by aircrew who fell into the sea rather than onto land during both World Wars led to the realisation that the most important thing to do is to cool the burn as soon as possible.

Put the affected area under cold water for ten minutes. If a child has been burned, don't let them get too cold.

After water, apply a clean, non-stick dressing. Clingfilm is a good option. Avoid cotton wool. The dressing prevents infection and cuts down the pain. DO NOT apply butter, oil or ointment. Don't burst the blisters; they prevent infection getting under the skin. Watch out for swelling and remove any rings if hands are burnt.

(Dr R. McConnell)
from www.studenthealth.co.uk/leaflets/BurnsAndScalds

When advising on personal problems, you will be making suggestions, exploring options, but advice such as that in Extract B, from an expert to the public, has to be *clear* and *factual*.

Two techniques used in Extract B are worth noting:

- The writer uses **imperative verbs** to convey advice and instruction. These are rather like commands: *Stand up straight! Don't do that!* They are usually at the beginnings of sentences. This may be a style of writing you use when describing a practical experiment in science.
- The writer **varies sentence length** effectively. The long second sentence, which is a sort of introduction, is followed by generally short sentences so that the information is conveyed clearly.

> **Activity 1.3c**   Identify the imperative verbs in Extract B. One has been underlined as an example.

Serious practice

> **UNIT ACTIVITY 1.3**   Write a report for your class tutor advising on measures to improve the environment in the classroom.

Hints

- Read the question carefully. Identify the words which refer to the purpose, form and audience.
- Look back to the other activities in this unit to see what techniques you could use. For example: use of *I* and *you*; strong statements of opinion; varied sentence length; use of signpost words and phrases.
- Use subheadings to organise your report (see the suggestions below).

WHAT EXAMINERS ARE LOOKING FOR

The grade A description for a task such as Unit Activity 1.3 would be:

'The report is powerful in its communication of relevant ideas, with confident awareness of the appropriate format.'

Compare this with the grade C description:

'The report conveys relevant ideas clearly, with sound awareness of the appropriate format.'

FORM, AUDIENCE AND PURPOSE

- The **form** of your writing is a report.
- The **audience** (or readership) is your class tutor.
- The **purpose** of your report is to advise.

TITLE AND SUBHEADINGS

Use a title and these subheadings to organise your report:

- **Title**: the purpose of report.
- **Introduction**: identifying the problem.

- **Courses of action**: a discussion of possible ways of improving the classroom environment, with a consideration of advantages and disadvantages, such as cost.
- **Recommendations**: your advice.

PLANNING YOUR WRITING

Look back to page 13 for a suggested way of generating ideas and then arranging them in a sensible order.

Use that technique here: first jot down ideas at random on a sheet of paper, then look for links between the ideas so that you can group them together into paragraphs.

Unit 1.4

Establishing a relationship with your reader

The unit activity is to write a speech and a letter (see page 21).

The Big Issue **magazine is a combination of hard-hitting journalism and writing about the world of arts and entertainment.**

THE BIG ISSUE

The inspiration for the magazine came from *Street News*, a newspaper sold by homeless people in New York.

The Big Issue campaigns on behalf of homeless and socially excluded people. Its street sellers (vendors) have been homeless themselves. They keep a proportion of the takings to provide them with an income. *The Big Issue* now sees its jobs, education and training service as its main focus in helping people move on from selling the magazine, within a wider context of tackling homelessness through understanding that the issues of health, housing and employment have to be addressed.

In 1999 the organisation helped 98 people into jobs, 3 to set up their own businesses, 15 took up voluntary work and 122 secured places on training schemes.

John Bird, founder of The Big Issue:

'Every now and then we get people who misinterpret *The Big Issue*. The latest of these was a group of councillors in Peterborough who wanted to see *The Big Issue* banned from the streets of their city. They said that people don't want to buy *The Big Issue* and that there are too many vendors.

But to ban *The Big Issue* would mean going to Parliament and getting the law of England changed. Also you would have to overturn the Pedlars Act of 1875, which states that publications can be distributed in the streets.

There is another mis-interpretation that the councillors of Peterborough should be reminded of. That is the nature of how *The Big Issue* works. Each *Big Issue* vendor has to buy their papers from us. They have to pay upfront. They have to look after their money. Unlike begging, they have to develop communication skills. They have to put time and effort into their selling. They cannot rely on us to give them handouts. In other words they have to work for their money.'

adapted from The Big Issue *website: www.bigissue.co.uk*

Making a start

Know your reader

In writing to argue, persuade and advise, you are trying to **influence** someone to your point of view or to a course of action. *You will succeed only if you know your intended reader.*

Sometimes you may know the reader personally. If, for example, you are asked to write a letter of advice to a friend, you would choose your style to suit someone you know well. But if you were writing to your headteacher, you would choose your words very differently. You may be asked to write for a readership of people you do not know, for example, the readers of the letters page in the local paper, or a group of visitors from a foreign country.

Having established the audience for your writing, you need to think about their probable point of view, their interests, their backgrounds. Only then can you find **common ground** with the people you are trying to influence.

Activity 1.4a

1 Imagine that you need to write a letter to each of the following people, influencing them to your point of view. What do you think would be an appropriate way of writing for each situation?
Make a copy of the table and choose words from the list to complete it.

Dear …	Most appropriate way of writing
Headteacher	
best friend	
your English class	
parent	
grandparent you rarely see	
local businessmen	

affectionate	emotional	formal	organised	warm
detached	factual	informal	sarcastic	witty

Read the extract opposite which is about *The Big Issue* magazine. You discover that some local councillors have proposed a ban on The Big Issue street vendors selling the magazine in your town. The council will be debating the ban in a week's time, and a vote will be taken. You would like to influence local opinion on this matter. You decide on two approaches:

• a speech to your class
• a letter to your local newspaper.

Read Unit Activity 1.4 on page 21.

Planning your speech

Activity 1.4b

Think about the audience for your speech. Write five adjectives which you think describe the kind of audience you will face.

Objection!

But surely all groups of people are made up of individuals, and it is wrong to stereotype a class or a newspaper's readership in this way? A class, for example, contains a great variety of types, views and values.

True, but when you write for a group of people, you do have to draw some conclusions about the group as a whole so that you can focus your arguments and choose an appropriate style.

Hint

Useful adjectives:

compassionate	middle-aged
easy-going	old
fun	rebellious
generous	scruffy
intolerant	stuffy
irresponsible	young
mean	

LETTER-WRITING
Each type, or genre, of writing has its own set of 'rules' or conventions. Look at your local newspaper's letter page:

◆ How long are the letters on average?
◆ How do they start?
◆ Do they give addresses and other details?
◆ How do the letter writers sign off at the end?
◆ Do they use any effective ways of opening and ending?
◆ Do some letters seem more effective than others in making their point? Why?

When you write your own letter to the local paper, try to include some of the points you have learnt above.

Organising your ideas

You have considered the values and interests of your class as an audience. You now need to use that knowledge to influence their thinking and their actions. Think of it in terms of fishing:

1 The bait!

How could you grab your audience's attention straightaway?

Activity 1.4c	Put these possible openings into order of effectiveness, and compare with others in the class:

● I believe that *The Big Issue* should be sold on our streets.
● Are you sitting comfortably? Warm? Had a good lunch? Looking forward to a good dinner?
● You've seen them. They smell and they look unhealthy. They try to push those magazines into your hands. They are no better than beggars really.

2 The hook!

Some in your audience may object to your arguments and resist you. You need to anticipate their arguments with your own counter-arguments.

Activity 1.4d	Think of some possible objections and how you will counter them. Copy and complete this table:

Objections to vendors	My counter-arguments
They spend their takings on drugs and drink.	Most are anxious to find work and training.

3 The strike!

Finally you will land your fish. To win your audience over completely you may need to use persuasive techniques such as **rhetorical questions** to give your argument **emotional appeal**, reinforced by **alliteration**, and present your audience with a stark choice, for example:

Do we want to live in a town where the poor and the excluded are driven away, or do we want to live in a caring and compassionate community which supports its fellow human beings who are down on their luck?

Planning your letter

Activity 1.4e	Think about the readership of your local newspaper.

● It is more difficult to generalise about them.
● You do not know them.
● You are addressing them in a public medium – the local newspaper – very different from your familiar classroom.
● Many of them will have strong views about 'beggars', crime and litter.

Write five adjectives to describe the readership. (The list on page 19 will help.)

Organising your ideas

Now start to think about the structure of your letter. Use the same approach as for your speech, but this time in letter format.

1 The bait!

A strong opening should address the issue directly, but should not antagonise the readers.

> **Activity 1.4f**   Write two possible opening sentences for your letter and compare with others in the class.

2 The hook!

Think about the types of argument that might be effective for this readership. They will probably need more convincing than your class.

> **Activity 1.4g**   Use information about *The Big Issue* to calm people's concerns about the vendors.

3 The strike!

This is where you can bring in a more emotional appeal to people's sense of humanity and compassion.

Serious practice

Now you have planned your speech and letter, complete the unit activity.

> **UNIT ACTIVITY 1.4**
> 1   Write a speech to the class in support of *The Big Issue* vendors.
> 2   Write a letter to the local newspaper in support of *The Big Issue* vendors.

WHAT EXAMINERS ARE LOOKING FOR

The mark scheme for tasks such as those in Unit Activity 1.4 would say that a successful answer will:

'create an appropriate register for a speech or a letter that will engage the attention and interest of the reader or listener.'

Register means the type of language you use in certain situations. How formal do you need to be? What level of knowledge and understanding do you expect your readers or listeners to have?

Hints

- Read the questions carefully. Identify the words which refer to the purpose, form and audience.
- Plan the sequence of paragraphs carefully.
- Read your writing through from the point of view of someone with a different point of view: how convincing and persuasive would you find your speech or letter?
- Try reading your speech aloud.
- Remember that a third of the marks will be awarded for accurate spelling and punctuation. Check carefully.

ESTABLISHING A RELATIONSHIP WITH YOUR READER: A SUMMARY

- Think about your audience
  - What are their concerns, values and attitudes?
  - How can you adjust the arguments you use and the way you write to meet their needs?

Find common ground
  - Meet your audience half way by finding points you can agree on.
  - Anticipate their arguments by having counter-arguments ready.
- Be aware of the conventions of different forms of writing, for example, letters, speeches (see also Unit 1.6).

Unit 1.5

Choosing the right style

The unit activity is to write a speech to your class (see page 25).

Extract

A

Were you as stunned as I was by the recently-reported juvenile crime figures? Well, the answer is you don't know. Because you don't know how stunned I was. But I can tell you. Very stunned. Shocked, surprised and amazed. Taken aback and utterly confounded. Really, really, very astonished indeed.
And before you start making excuses on behalf of young people. Or saying that you personally had expected to see a significant rise in reported crime blah blah, let us be clear. Let us be clear what happened between 1980 and 1990.

There has been a substantial decrease in recorded juvenile crime over the past decade. The number of juveniles aged under 17 convicted of or cautioned for indictable offences fell by 37 per cent.
You can now see the cause of my bogglement. I read all that stuff in the papers about young lawlessness. The moral vacuum (nothing to do with Hoover, apparently). Not knowing the difference between right and … (sorry, I forget the name of the other thing … just slipped my mind).

from an article by Mick Sturbs in Young People Now

Making a start

It's a matter of choice

Your style of writing is formed by the words you choose. You may choose to be very formal and correct, or at the other end of the scale very informal, using colloquial expressions and slang.

How do you choose an appropriate style?

Your knowledge of your **audience**, and your **purpose** for writing, give you information about how formal you need to be. Look at the two examples, Extracts A and B.

Extract A is the beginning of an article in a magazine called *Young People Now*. It is the writer's reaction to the news that juvenile crime had decreased in the previous decade.

What are the features of the style of writing in Extract A? It is written in an informal, **colloquial** style. Colloquial means the language of everyday conversation, and you can see how the writer tries to imitate this by using half-sentences, false starts, repetition and slang expressions.

Extract B uses a very different style of writing. It is the beginning of a speech by President John F. Kennedy to the American people on 20 January 1961, on the occasion of his inauguration as President of the United States.

Extract B

Fellow citizens, we observe today not a victory of party, but a celebration of freedom – symbolising an end, as well as a beginning – signifying renewal as well as change. For I have sworn before you and Almighty God the same solemn oath our forbears prescribed nearly a century and three quarters ago.

The world is very different now. For man holds in his mortal hands the power to abolish all forms of human poverty and all forms of human life. And yet the same revolutionary beliefs for which our forbears fought are still at issue around the globe – the belief that the rights of man come not from the generosity of the state, but from the hand of God.

We dare not forget today that we are the heirs of that first revolution. Let the word go forth from this time and place, to friend and foe alike, that the torch has been passed to a new generation of Americans – born in this century, tempered by war, disciplined by a hard and bitter peace, proud of our ancient heritage – and unwilling to witness or permit the slow undoing of those human rights to which this Nation has always been committed, and to which we are committed today at home and around the world.

Let every nation know, whether it wishes us well or ill, that we shall pay any price, bear any burden, meet any hardship, support any friend, oppose any foe, in order to assure the survival and the success of liberty …

… And so, my fellow Americans, ask not what your country can do for you – ask what you can do for your country.

My fellow citizens of the world, ask not what America will do for you, but what together we can do for the freedom of man.

from www.barteby.com

A STYLE FOR EVERY OCCASION

For success at GCSE you need to be able to adopt different styles for different purposes, for example:

- a letter applying for a job
  - Your **purpose** here is to be clear and informative in putting a case for yourself.

- Your **audience**, a potential employer, might well judge you partly on the standard of your written English.
- A suitable **style** will therefore be quite formal and grammatically correct. This does not mean that the style has to be stiff and artificial; it needs to express certain aspects of your personality, so there can still be humour and individuality.

- a letter to a friend describing a holiday
  - Your **purpose** here is to amuse and entertain.
  - Your **audience**, a friend, will not judge you on the accuracy of your grammar.
  - A suitable **style** will therefore be colloquial and humorous. It may well be full of slang expressions, private jokes and bizarre punctuation.

KEY WORDS

colloquial
The language of everyday conversation, for example, *really, really very astonished indeed*. There is no slang here, but it is deliberately written to imitate ordinary conversation rather than standard written English.

A colloquial expression is a **colloquialism**.

slang
Non-standard English used very informally, normally in speech. It is sometimes a kind of private language to exclude outsiders, such as Cockney rhyming slang, gangster slang or playground slang. If the writer of the article had written *gobsmacked* rather than *astonished*, that would have been slang

Activity 1.5a

1   Find examples of the following style features in Extract A:
a) words or phrases which you think are colloquial or slang
b) grammatically incorrect sentences (sentences without verbs)
c) repetition
d) humour or irony
e) exaggeration.

2   Discuss as a class:
a) Do you think this style of writing is suitable for a published article about juvenile crime?
b) Do you think the writer judged his audience accurately (*Young People Now*) and wrote in a way that would appeal to that section of the population?

How is the style of Extract B different from the style of Extract A? Look at:

- the words chosen – old-fashioned vocabulary (these words would have sounded old-fashioned in 1961 too)
- unusual or old-fashioned word order (**syntax**). For example, he uses *Ask not* rather than the usual expression *Don't ask.*

Activity 1.5b

1   a) Find examples in the speech of old-fashioned vocabulary.
b) What is the effect of using such vocabulary?

2   a) Find examples in the speech of solemn, impressive-sounding sentences.
b) Why does he use these?

HISTORICAL CONTEXT

A speech is delivered at a particular moment in history to a particular audience for a particular effect.

To understand the full impact of John F. Kennedy's speech, you need to know the historical context. You will then understand the hopes and fears of the American people at that moment in time.

- In 1961, the Second World War was still fresh in people's memories.
- There were two super powers, the United States and the Soviet Union, each representing a different way of governing a country – democracy and communism.
- Many people thought that these two super powers were bound to go to war at some point as they struggled to gain influence over other countries.

- If there was a war, it would involve nuclear weapons.
- The future in 1961 seemed uncertain and dangerous to many Americans.

Other aspects of style found in the speech include:

- **The use of opposites, or contrasts** The term for this is **antithesis**: a figure of speech in which thoughts or words are balanced in contrast, for example, *For man holds in his mortal hands the power to abolish all forms of human poverty and all forms of human life.* Here the repeated phrase *all forms* highlights the contrast between the human race's potential for good and its potential for self-destruction.
- **Alliteration** This tends to make a phrase memorable to a listener, for example, *to friend and foe alike.* That is why it is common in advertising and newspaper headlines.
- **Lists** Linking similar ideas in lists is a common feature of speeches.
- **Metaphors** A metaphor can turn a vague idea into a clear, visual image.

Activity 1.5c

1 Find examples in the speech of:
   a) antithesis
   b) alliteration
   c) lists.
2 Why are lists effective in speeches?
3 *Torch* is used in this passage as a metaphor. What idea does it represent?
4 Which words in the list below best describe the style of this passage?

artificial	conversational	heightened	pompous
authoritative	dramatic	impressive	powerful
colloquial	emotional	persuasive	slangy

5 Is the style suitable to the occasion? Consider the purpose of this speech and the audience.

Serious practice

UNIT ACTIVITY 1.5 You have been elected class captain. Write your inaugural speech to be delivered to your class. Start with *Fellow students,* …

 TECHNIQUES YOU COULD USE IN YOUR SPEECH

Antithesis

- *Fellow students, ask not what this school can do for you, but what you can do for this school.*
- *We could as a class succeed in reducing litter; we could equally say 'It's the cleaner's job', and ignore the problem.*

Lists

- *I have three aims: to reduce the litter in the classroom; to raise money for a local charity; to provide a secure locker for each member of the class.*

Metaphor and alliteration

- *Parents pull us one way; our friends pull us another --- it is not easy to follow a straight path towards our goals.*

WHAT EXAMINERS ARE LOOKING FOR

How accurate is your spelling? Grade C standard of spelling is 'mostly correct, but may contain occasional errors'. Grade A standard of spelling is 'consistently excellent'.

Hints

- Read the question carefully. Identify the words which refer to the purpose, form and audience.
- Set out your priorities for the year, the problems ahead and how you intend to tackle them.
- Your aim is to have the class working together as a team working towards common goals, so you should appeal to a sense of loyalty and community.
- Write in a formal style using some of the techniques from the speech by John F. Kennedy. You could even adapt some of his sentences to your own purposes.
- Your speech need not be very serious in content — it is an exercise in writing in a certain style and using certain techniques.

Unit 1.6

Forms of writing

The unit activity is to write a magazine article exploring an issue (see page 29).

Extract **A**

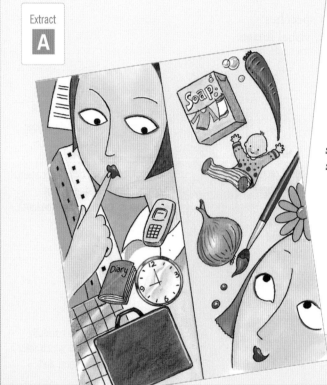

Happy at Home

Sir

Why is there a constant assumption that a woman who chooses to stay at home should be an object of derision and pity?

I have been in the fortunate position to be able to choose to be a full-time mother since the birth of my two daughters, now aged nine and eight years old. I spend very little time worrying about our choice of soap powder. It only takes a few hours a week to keep our small house clean, which leaves me free to pursue my many interests which include art, creative embroidery, cultivating an allotment and serving as a school governor.

It is my working friends, over-worked and stressed, who lose out. I have my freedom.

from The Independent, *2 May 1996*

Making a start

Sometimes examination questions simply say *Write an essay …* or *Write about …*, but often they require a particular **form** of writing, for example:

*   *Write a **speech** for a class debate …*
*   *Write an **article** for a school magazine …*
*   *Write a **letter** to the local paper …*
*   *Write the wording of a **leaflet** ….*

You should make yourself familiar with the various forms of writing which you might have to write in an examination. Each form has its own conventions (or rules). These are not hard and fast rules – they are readers' expectations of the style and layout of, for example, a formal letter or a tabloid newspaper article.

Letter-writing

Technology has made letter-writing less common and, some would say, less important than in the past. However, GCSE students are still expected to be able to write well-structured letters for different purposes and audiences.

Extract A is an example of a letter to a newspaper.

Activity 1.6a

1 How has the writer of Extract A used paragraphs to organise her ideas?
2 How does she use personal experience to support her ideas?
3 How does she use sentence length to provide an effective ending?

LETTER-WRITING IN THE EXAM

Addresses

Unless the question specifically asks for it, do not write addresses in examination answers. Start with the salutation.

The salutation: *Dear …*

This is the polite form of words used to open the letter. It should be used even if the writer is angry and does not regard the recipient as a dear friend at all!

- Use *Dear Sir/Madam* for a formal letter where you do not know the recipient personally.

- Use *Dear Mrs Smith* if you are given a name, but the person is not an acquaintance.
- Use *Dear Dave* for an informal letter to a friend.

The ending

Signing-off a letter can cause confusion, but the 'rules' are not as strict as they once were.

- *Dear Sir/Madam* is usually signed off with *Yours faithfully*, then the first and surname of the writer.
- *Dear Mrs Smith* is usually signed off with *Yours sincerely*, then the first and surname of the writer.

- *Dear Dave* would have a less formal signing off such as *Yours* or *See you soon*, then the first name of the writer.

There is no penalty for the signing-off unless the writer ignores the purpose of the letter. For example, a formal letter of job application which ended with *See ya* would be inappropriately informal and would not impress the recipient – or the examiner.

The marks for letter-writing are largely awarded for an appropriate style, for awareness of the audience, for paragraph organisation and for accuracy of spelling and punctuation. The details of openings and endings are less important than these aspects.

Speeches

Speeches have a live audience. If you are asked to write a speech, you need to show awareness of the audience and to take their needs into consideration. Your listeners have only one chance to hear your arguments. You have to help them to follow your point of view by using a range of techniques.

Extract B is from a political speech. For another example, see the extract from John F. Kennedy's speech on page 23.

Extract B

The one public service we all use all the time is the streets where we live. And in too many places, streets and public spaces have become dirty, ugly and dangerous.

Britain needs to feel proud of its public spaces, not ashamed. We need to make it safer for children to walk or cycle to school in safety. We need local parks which are well looked after and easily reached with a pushchair. We need streets to be free of litter, dog mess and mindless vandalism ….

To deliver this we have to tackle the small concerns, which can turn into big problems. It is important that we break the sense of fatalism about parts of our public sphere – everywhere we can make a start will make a difference.

That is why we are addressing low-level crime and disorder and local environmental degradation alongside serious crime and pollution ….

Health, education, crime and the economy will continue to be people's top concerns. They will remain our top priorities. But that must go hand-in-hand with improving our local quality of life and strengthening our communities.

We have made a start but there is plenty more to do.

from a speech by
Prime Minister Tony Blair, 1999

WRITING A SPEECH IN THE EXAM

The opening
Start your speech with a salutation, such as:

◆ *Fellow students, ...*
◆ *Members of the local youth council, ...*

This signals immediately that you are aware that you are writing a speech for an audience.

Activity 1.6b Look at the persuasive techniques used in Extract B. Find examples of the use of:
a) *we* and *our* to suggest agreement between the speaker and the audience
b) repeated phrases to give the speech shape
c) different sentence lengths to give variety to the ear
d) lists
e) balanced sentences with contrasting parts.

Newspaper or magazine articles

You might be asked to write in a journalistic style in order to explore an issue or to present individuals and their views. Extract C is an example of a magazine article.

Extract
C

The Other Side of the Wall

How a prison sentence forced a young man to change his life and build a future

By Angela Neustatter

There are two memories that Shehwar believes will always be there in his head as 'a warning and a guidance'. One is of the moment when his mother, sitting in court and hearing her son sentenced, broke down in tears. 'I wanted more than anything in the world to comfort her, but, of course, I had done this to her.' The second is also of his mother but this time 'she was smiling and laughing – so happy'. It was the day she visited him in prison and he told her he had won a place at Sunderland University, and that he would be going there when he finished his sentence.

Shehwar relates this sitting in a burger bar, munching his way through a baconburger and chips. He talks rapidly, eyes bright, long fingers gesturing in the air as he explains a point. He has the wiry nervousness of someone who is not certain they are acceptable even though in 1998, while in prison, he won Jack Straw's Personality of the Year award for the enormous effort he had made to change his life. 'It made me look back on my life and see what a destructive path I had been on'.

from the Telegraph Magazine,
22 April 2000

Activity 1.6c Find these features of a magazine article in Extract C:
a) a headline and sub-headline – How do they differ?
b) the opening – What type of opening is this?
c) the use of quotations or interviews
d) the use of contrast between the two memories
e) human interest – How does the writer involve us in details about the young person's appearance and experiences?

**WRITING AN ARTICLE
IN THE EXAM**

Start with a headline
This shows your awareness of the form of writing. Your choice of headline will show your knowledge of headline language and give clues about the type of publication this is supposed to be.

Use of **puns** or **alliteration** in headlines is effective. For example, a headline used for an article about banning cars from a city centre was: *Where carfree means carefree.*

In an examination you are not expected to spend time on the **layout**. There are no marks awarded for visual presentation. Do not write in columns or draw pictures.

Serious practice

UNIT ACTIVITY 1.6 Write a magazine article in response to **one** of the following.

Either:

1 Tony Blair's speech.
   Your article should be about how your local environment could be improved for the benefit of the community, referring to the ideas in the speech.

Or:

2 The letter to *The Independent*.
   Your article should explore the role of women in modern society, using the views expressed in the letter as a starting point.

> **Hint**
>
> Read the question carefully. Identify the words which refer to purpose, form and audience.

> **WHAT EXAMINERS ARE LOOKING FOR**
>
> In all tasks, examiners will look for 'a clear focus on relevant issues', and whether you are able to 'adapt writing for particular purposes and audiences' – in this case, an article for a magazine.

OTHER FORMS OF WRITING
In the exam you might be asked to write in other forms, for example:

◆ **Leaflets**
Do not spend time on layout or format in an examination. You might be asked to provide the *wording* for a leaflet, but there would be no marks for layout or artwork. See Unit 1.10 for practice in leaflet writing.

◆ **Reports**
See Unit 1.3 for information and tips about report writing.

Unit 1.7

Planning your writing

The unit activity is to produce a mind map and a paragraph plan (see page 33).

Making a start

Plan to succeed

You will not achieve a good mark for your writing if you do not plan. Markers of GCSE English examinations are instructed to reward answers that are 'consciously shaped'. This means the answers have a **structure**, a **paragraph plan**, and that ideas are in a **logical order**.

If you are producing a piece of writing for coursework, you can plan thoroughly, draft and redraft. But if you have to write an argument in an examination in about 40 minutes, you do not have long to plan. You need to have some planning techniques to hand, and you need to practise them so that they become second nature. You can then tackle writing tasks under timed conditions with confidence.

For example, let's take a typical task:

'It is better to be an only child than to have several brothers and sisters.'
Argue for or against this statement.

Brainstorming

This is a useful way of collecting ideas for a piece of writing. Ideas on the topic, either for or against the proposition, are jotted down randomly with no attempt to sort them into any order. A brainstorm for the question above might produce these points:

<u>Single children</u>

Receive more individual attention

Learn quickly how to get on with adults

Find it harder to develop relationships with their peers

May be spoilt by presents and treats

Develop a wide network of friends outside the home

Expect to have their own way

Find it more difficult to learn about how to resolve conflict, and the meaning of compromise, sharing, give and take

Don't have role models from older siblings, or the responsibility of caring for younger ones

Are self-sufficient

Can be lonely and isolated

Activity 1.7a   Add some ideas of your own or from group discussion to the brainstorm.

THE STAGES OF
PLANNING

1   Generate ideas by
    brainstorming or producing
    a mind map
2   Edit ideas
3   Produce a paragraph plan

Mind maps

Mind maps are a development of brainstorming. They have the same purpose – to generate ideas on a topic and organise them into a persuasive argument.

Some people prefer mind maps to basic brainstorming because mind maps show **links** and **connections** between ideas and help you to arrange your ideas more effectively.

A mind map is produced by first writing the **topic**, or main idea, in the centre of the page and then writing the associated ideas around the topic with lines showing how the ideas are linked, starting from the central topic and working outwards in all directions. An organised structure of key words and images emerges. Many people find this a more creative approach, with new ideas and approaches being generated. See the example below.

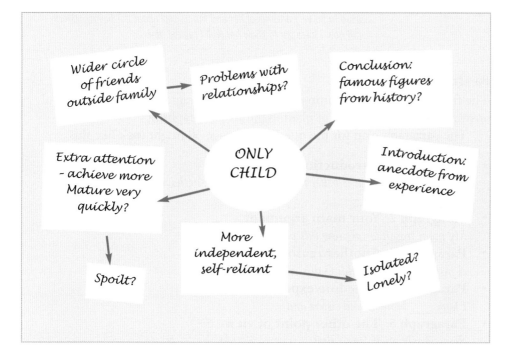

MIND MAPS ARE USEFUL TOOLS FOR MAKING NOTES IN ALL SUBJECTS

◆ They can be a mixture of words, images, symbols.
◆ They work because they reflect the way the brain works, i.e. not just in a straight line, but by associating one idea with another, comparing and linking as it goes.

◆ They highlight key words because they show in a **visual form** how a lesser idea, or detail, hangs on a larger, key idea.
◆ They are a revision tool because your visual memory will recall a mind map more readily than a list of words or phrases. This is particularly true if you use colour, arrows, outlining and other visual features to link associated ideas.

Editing your ideas

Some ideas might be rejected (crossed out); others might be sorted into *For* or *Against* (use ticks and crosses); the remaining ideas can then be sorted into a logical order (use numbers).

***

Activity 1.7b   Edit the results of the brainstorm on page 30.

1. Decide whether you are *for* or *against* the statement in the question.
2. Use ticks and crosses to sort the views into *for* and *against*.
3. Decide on the best order to give your overall argument a logical development. Don't forget to use opposing arguments in order to demolish them!
4. You do not want one-sentence paragraphs, so group the views into just a few paragraphs.
5. Add any anecdotes from your or others' experiences which will add impact to your argument by illustrating your views. For example, *I am the middle child of three brothers. Although we do argue continually, there are benefits to a larger family, such as …* or *My friend is an only child. I used to be very envious of her and fantasised about not having sisters, but now I have got to know her well I realise that …*

***

Paragraph plan

The final stage in your planning is to produce a paragraph plan. A successful answer will show evidence of planning in its paragraphing.

The paragraph plan for the question on page 30 might look like this:

- **Paragraph 1: Introduction**
  I want to argue that it is better to (be an only child, or, have several brothers and sisters).
- **Paragraph 2: Your main argument**
  My <u>main reason</u> for arguing this point of view is …
- **Paragraph 3: Another reason (optional)**
  A <u>further reason</u> for holding this view is …
- **Paragraph 4: Anecdote/experience**
  I have ___ brothers and sisters and …
- **Paragraph 5: The other point of view**
  <u>*Some people might argue that …*</u>
- **Paragraph 6: Conclusion**
  <u>*Therefore*</u> *I think I have shown that…*

Note the words and phrases above which are underlined. Look back to the signpost words in Unit 1.3. The underlined words are also signposts for the reader. They help to link the ideas and guide the reader from one point to the next. We will look at them in greater detail in Unit 1.9.

This basic paragraph plan can be applied to most argument assignments. It would need to be adjusted, however, for a writing to advise assignment.

***

Activity 1.7c   Use the model above to write a paragraph plan for this question:

Write advice to parents who are concerned about their teenage children arguing all the time.

***

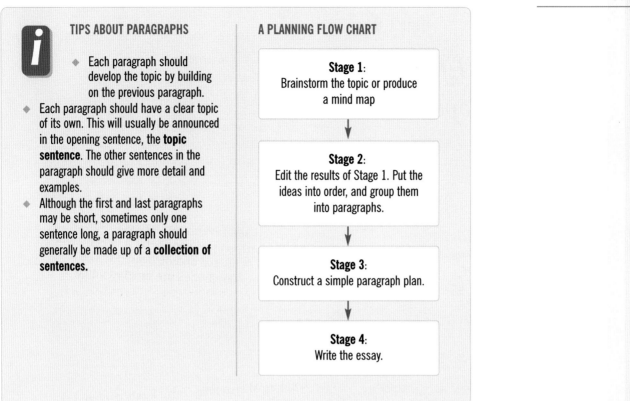

TIPS ABOUT PARAGRAPHS

- Each paragraph should develop the topic by building on the previous paragraph.
- Each paragraph should have a clear topic of its own. This will usually be announced in the opening sentence, the **topic sentence**. The other sentences in the paragraph should give more detail and examples.
- Although the first and last paragraphs may be short, sometimes only one sentence long, a paragraph should generally be made up of a **collection of sentences.**

A PLANNING FLOW CHART

Stage 1:
Brainstorm the topic or produce a mind map

↓

Stage 2:
Edit the results of Stage 1. Put the ideas into order, and group them into paragraphs.

↓

Stage 3:
Construct a simple paragraph plan.

↓

Stage 4:
Write the essay.

Serious practice

UNIT ACTIVITY 1.7 Choose **one** of these questions.

Either:

1 Write your response to the title we have been considering in this unit:

'It is better to be an only child than to have several brothers and sisters'. Argue for or against this statement.

The planning for this has been largely done for you, but you should practise a brainstorm or a mind map anyway, using ideas from the unit plus your own ideas. You can use the example paragraph plan.

Or:

2 For a greater challenge, take a new topic and practise the procedure from scratch:

'Students in the final year of GCSE should not do part-time work.' Argue for or against this statement.

Generate ideas with a brainstorm or a mind map, produce a paragraph plan, and write your response.

WHAT EXAMINERS ARE LOOKING FOR
In all tasks, examiners will reward writing which has a 'clear structure supported by effective paragraphing'.

The planning procedure described in this unit has only one purpose: to help the reader follow your argument and so be convinced by your ideas. You will become a more effective writer if your work is properly organised.

Unit 1.8

Effective openings

The unit activity is to write an article with an effective opening
(see page 37)

(see page 37)

Extract
A

I want to begin this New Year's message by thanking those people in the public services unable to spend the New Year holiday with their family.

Extract
B

Four score and seven years ago our fathers brought forth on this continent, a new nation, conceived in liberty, and dedicated to the proposition that all men are created equal.

Extract
C

My loving people, we have been persuaded by some, that are careful of our safety, to take heed how we commit ourselves to armed multitudes, for fear of treachery; but I assure you, I do not desire to live to distrust my faithful and loving people.

Extract
D

London. Michaelmas Term lately over and the Lord Chancellor sitting in Lincoln's Inn Hall. Implacable November weather. As much mud in the streets, as if the waters had but newly retired from the face of the earth, and it would not be wonderful to meet a megalosaurus, forty feet long or so, waddling like an elephantine lizard up Holborn Hill.

Extract
E

One morning, as Gregor Samsa was waking from anxious dreams, he discovered that in bed he had been changed into a monstrous verminous insect.

Extract
F

Friends, Romans, countrymen, lend me your ears.

Making a start

First impressions

The opening sets the tone for the rest of the piece of writing. Here are some openings to letters:

Dear _____

1   *I was disgusted to read that the council intends …*
2   *I am interested in the post advertised in last week's …*
3   *A boy! I don't believe it! That is brilliant news …*
4   *My son was told by Mrs Watts, his History teacher, that his appearance is a disgrace.*
    What right does this person have …
5   *I am so sorry about the misunderstanding …*
6   *I am writing on behalf of my client, Dodgy Debt Collectors, to advise you that …*
7   *I was outraged by the bad language on last Saturday's programme …*

Activity 1.8a   1   With a partner, find an adjective or two to describe the tone you would expect from the rest of each letter. Angry? Excited? Apologetic? Formal? Use these adjectives and think of others.
2   What do you think is the subject or purpose of each letter?

So, just the opening few words can give the reader a lot of clues about the sort of letter this is going to be. First impressions are important!

Different ways of starting a piece of writing

Imagine a student is writing a speech arguing for the proposition:

Dogs are a public nuisance and their numbers should be strictly controlled.

The student jots down various ways of starting the speech, trying to find the most effective. See the table below.

Activity 1.8b   1   Link each opening in the left-hand column of the table with the types of opening on the right which best describe it, for example, 2 – d. There may be more than one answer in some cases.
2   Now decide with a partner which opening you think grabs the reader's or listener's attention most effectively. Compare your views with others in the class.

Possible openings		Types of opening
1	Dogs. Cuddly and affectionate pets, or potentially vicious health hazards?	a Anecdote; personal experience
2	I strongly believe that dogs should be banned from most public places.	b Head-on challenge to the audience
3	Have you ever considered how much dog waste is produced daily?	c Statement of fact
4	Dog owners are not known for their clear thinking about their furry friends.	d Rhetorical question to involve audience
5	There are ten million dogs in this country. I sometimes think they all bark together at night outside my house.	e Appealing to common ground with your opponents
6	Would all you dog owners out there raise your hand?	f Sarcastic tone
7	Each year hundreds of people are injured by uncontrolled dangerous dogs.	g Use of humour
8	I sometimes think dog owners are barking mad.	h Straight statement of opinion
9	I own a dog myself – a little Yorkshire terrier – but I am sometimes appalled at the behaviour of other dog owners.	i Both sides of argument presented
10	I once tried to stroke a bulldog, having been assured by its owner that 'it wouldn't hurt a fly'.	j Exaggeration for effect
		k Shock tactics

Many of you will have dogs and will disagree with the opinions expressed in the table. Now is your chance to respond.

> **Activity 1.8c**
> 1   Write five possible openings for a speech opposing the proposition that 'Dogs are a public nuisance'. In other words, you are *defending* dog ownership. Use ideas from the 'Types of opening' column in the table, and make sure each is different in approach.
> 2   Compare your ideas with others in the class.

What conclusions can you draw about effective openings?

Is it better to play safe and simply state a point of view without trying to be too clever or gimmicky, for example, *I believe that dogs should be more strictly controlled*? Or should you take chances and show off your range of writing skills with a more startling opening?

As ever, you should be guided by the **context** of the writing:

- What is the purpose of this piece of writing?
- What is the form?
- Who is it for?

If you consider those basic questions beforehand, you should avoid an opening which is inappropriate.

First and foremost you should aim to engage the reader's interest immediately. All your clever reasoning and evidence can come later. If the reader is not interested in the first few sentences, it will all go to waste anyway!

> **Activity 1.8d**   Look at the well-known openings to speeches and novels in Extracts A–F.
> 1   Who do you think wrote each one? Try to match them with the following people:
>
> | | |
> |---|---|
> | Charles Dickens | Queen Elizabeth 1 |
> | Tony Blair | William Shakespeare |
> | Abraham Lincoln | Franz Kafka |
>
> 2   Which openings grab your attention? Why?

Look at the following two openings. Extract G is from the beginning of an article attacking school sports.

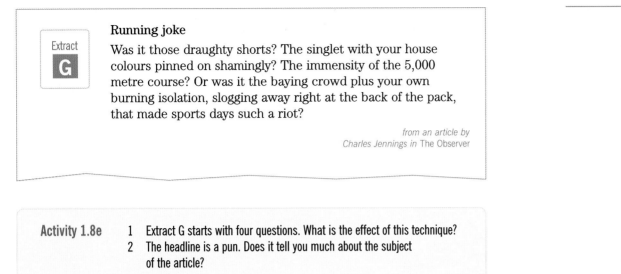

Extract **G**

Running joke

Was it those draughty shorts? The singlet with your house colours pinned on shamingly? The immensity of the 5,000 metre course? Or was it the baying crowd plus your own burning isolation, slogging away right at the back of the pack, that made sports days such a riot?

*from an article by
Charles Jennings in* The Observer

Activity 1.8e

1 Extract G starts with four questions. What is the effect of this technique?
2 The headline is a pun. Does it tell you much about the subject of the article?

Extract H is the beginning of an article about an environmental campaigner.

Extract **H**

The day I broke my car habit

This month, I think I'll have a party. I will commission a cake in the shape of a mangled vehicle. For I have something special to celebrate. Ten years ago I took one of the best decisions I have ever made. I got rid of my car.

from an article by George Monbiot in
The Guardian, *15 September 1999*

Activity 1.8f

1 The headline in Extract H explains the topic of the article. To what does the headline compare car ownership?
2 What is the effect of the short final sentence?

Serious practice

UNIT ACTIVITY 1.8 Choose **one** of these statements:

● 'School sports should not be compulsory'
● 'There are too many cars on our roads'.

1 Decide whether you wish to argue *for* or *against* your chosen topic.
2 Write **three** possible headlines to an article arguing your point of view.
3 Write **three** possible openings for the article.
4 Compare your headlines and openings with a partner and choose the most effective.
5 Now write the whole article. Before you start, remember what you have learnt about planning techniques.

WHAT EXAMINERS ARE LOOKING FOR

In judging the overall effectiveness of a piece of writing, examiners look at the opening to see how the topic is introduced to the reader.

Hints

◆ Read the question carefully. Identify the words which refer to purpose, form and audience.
◆ Try to avoid the obvious: *I believe there are too many cars on the road.* Look back through this unit to find different, more imaginative ways of starting.

Unit 1.9

Developing your writing

The unit activity is to write a speech using signpost words and phrases to link ideas (see page 41).

 Essay **A**

I think space exploration is a waste of money.

There are millions of starving people in this world but millions of dollars are spent on space travel.

All the money spent on space travel would build many hospitals and schools. Why don't we sort out this world first before trying to find another one?

All that has been achieved by space exploration is some moon rock and a lot of junk floating around in space. Several astronauts have been killed.

So I think I have shown that space travel is not worth the millions spent on it.

Essay **B**

To boldly go …, as Star Trek always starts, sums up the spirit of adventure and discovery that has led the human race to explore new worlds. I believe that this adventurous spirit is a good thing, and that space is indeed the 'final frontier' that we have to explore.

Space exploration is expensive. It is true that what the United States spends on rocket development could alleviate suffering around the world. Surely poverty and starvation should be tackled before the luxury of putting a man on Mars? Surely it is a selfish fantasy to ignore problems on our own doorstep on earth and indulge in science fiction adventures?

This is undoubtedly a strong argument, but it ignores human nature – our sense of adventure and our need to discover. Without this, how would America have been discovered? Without this, how would scientific and medical advances have been possible?

Without this, the human race would be scraping a Stone-Age existence.

Therefore, I oppose the proposition that space exploration is a waste of money. I hope I have convinced you that space exploration is exciting and that the scientific advances made by the space industry are important. The discoveries we will make in the future, both scientific and about other worlds, surely justify the expense.

Making a start

In Unit 1.7, you looked at ways of planning your work: brainstorms, mind maps and paragraph plans. In Unit 1.8, you considered how to write an effective opening. In this unit you will be looking at how to **develop your ideas**, how to flesh out the skeleton of your paragraph plan, and how to build on your opening.

Some common faults with writing to argue, persuade and advise include:

- essays running out of ideas after a promising start, and the writing becoming repetitive
- paragraphs being like a list of separate points, with few links between them
- ideas not following logically one to the other, so that the overall argument is unclear.

Essays A and B argue different points of view on the statement:
'Money spent on space exploration would be better spent on problems in this world.'

Activity 1.9a

1 Do these essays have the qualities listed in the table? Copy the table. Discuss the qualities with a partner, then put a tick or cross in the boxes in the table.

Qualities	Essay A	Essay B
There is an effective opening.		
Each paragraph has a topic which is developed.		
There are signpost words and phrases to link the ideas.		
There are persuasive techniques, such as repetition for effect and rhetorical questions.		
There are examples to expand and illustrate the arguments.		
The ending does more than repeat the opening.		
The whole argument is convincing.		

2 List some of the words from Essay B which show a higher level of vocabulary than Essay A.

WRITING IN THE EXAM

Write with conviction

Clearly Essay B is a more satisfactory answer than Essay A, but it is by no means perfect. For example, look again at the last paragraph of Essay B: does the writer actually do what is claimed? Sometimes something written with conviction can convince us even though the actual arguments used are not that strong!

Vocabulary and spelling

Your vocabulary, the words you choose, is an important aspect of the marks awarded for your GCSE writing tasks.

A third of the marks in all writing tasks are devoted to accurate spelling and punctuation. The mark for spelling is related to the range of words you use. You will achieve a higher mark if you use a more interesting and varied vocabulary, even if you make the occasional spelling error. There is nothing to be gained by playing safe, using a narrow range of words and making no spelling errors.

Developing ideas – be logical

*'After I did so well at Art GCSE, it seemed **logical** to study it for A-Level.'*

A successful essay in writing to argue, persuade, advise will flow **logically** from one idea to the next. The study of sound reasoning is called **logic**. When you are arguing a point of view in an essay, logic means: does the conclusion I have drawn follow from the arguments I have used? For example:

> **Fact:** It rained 20 days in September.
> **Fact:** There was a flu epidemic in September.
> **Conclusion:** Rain causes flu.

What comments would you make about the conclusion drawn from the above facts? Is there a **logical flaw**, or is the conclusion **valid**? Are there other factors which should be taken into account?

A possible response to this conclusion might be that two things occurring at the same time are not necessarily linked. There will be other factors causing the flu epidemic – such as what?

THE LIAR PARADOX

Logic has fascinated philosophers for thousands of years.

A philosopher from Crete, Epimenides, once stated: 'All Cretans are liars'. Since he was a Cretan himself, what are we to make of this statement? If it is true, then Epimenides must be a liar and his statement is therefore false. If Epimenides's statement is false, then his statement is true.

This sort of logical word puzzle is known as a **paradox**: a puzzle which seems to contradict itself and goes in circles.

Here is another paradoxical statement:

The following sentence is true; the previous sentence is false.

Activity 1.9b   A conclusion has been drawn from each set of facts below. With a partner, comment on whether the conclusion seems to be logically sound, or whether there is a flaw in the reasoning.

1   **Fact**: More footballers were sent off last season than ever before.
   Fact: There was an increase in crowd trouble last season.
   Conclusion: Trouble on the pitch lead to trouble off it.

2   **Fact**: Supermarket sales are rising.
   Fact: Fewer people use markets and small shops to buy food.
   Conclusion: The food sold at supermarkets is better than that sold in other outlets.

3   **Fact**: Light coloured cars have fewer accidents.
   Fact: The most popular car colours are dark.
   Conclusion: All cars should be white by law.

4   **Fact**: Buses in central London are crowded.
   Fact: People can stand for short journeys.
   Conclusion: Seats should be removed from buses.

5   **Fact**: Children watch more television these days.
   Fact: Juvenile crime is rising.
   Conclusion: Television causes crime.

Linking ideas

Signpost words and phrases, or discourse markers, were introduced in Unit 1.3. Now you need to become familiar with a wider range of signposts to use in your writing. Look at the signpost words opposite.

How to use signposts

People often make errors when using signpost words. These may be to do with:

- sentence structure
- punctuation.

Sentence structure

What is wrong with these statements?

- *Because space travel is very expensive.*
- *Although there have been many scientific advances from space exploration.*

Neither statement is a proper sentence because neither makes sense on its own. Compare them with:

- *Because space travel is very expensive, few countries can afford a space programme.*
- *Although there have been many scientific advances from space exploration, these advances are outweighed by the risks.*

These are proper sentences – they make complete sense on their own.

Punctuation

Where you use an adverb at the beginning of a sentence you should isolate it with a comma, for example:

- *Naturally, …*
- *Undoubtedly, …*
- *Obviously, …*
- *Alternatively, ….*

Adverbial phrases should also be separated by a comma, for example:

- *On the other hand, …*
- *For instance, …*
- *In conclusion, ….*

Serious practice

> **UNIT ACTIVITY 1.9** Write an essay arguing for or against space exploration based on the statement:
>
> Money spent on space exploration would be better spent on problems in this world.

MORE SIGNPOST WORDS AND PHRASES

To compare different ideas:
On the other hand
However
Whereas
In contrast
Although
Alternatively
Despite
Alternatively

To link similar ideas:
Similarly
Not only … but also
Furthermore
Likewise

To illustrate ideas:
For example
Such as
As shown by
For instance

To show cause and effect:
Because
Consequently
As a result

To summarise ideas:
Overall
Generally
In short
Therefore
In conclusion

WHAT EXAMINERS ARE LOOKING FOR

Mark schemes state that effective answers will 'convey to the reader persuasive ideas and arguments', in this case about space exploration. In other words, a series of reasons which contribute towards a convincing case.

> ### Hints
>
> - You can refer to the two essays on this topic in this unit if you wish.
> - Try to include evidence or information from other sources where possible. The Internet would help you with this.
> - Try to develop a logical argument over three to four paragraphs, each idea building on the one before.
> - Use signpost words and phrases from the lists above to link your ideas.
> - Remember what you have learnt from previous units about effective openings and planning.

Unit 1.10

Writing technique: language and layout

The unit activity is to write a leaflet using linguistic (language) and presentational (layout) devices (see page 45).

Example

A

Will you give 10p a day £3 a month to help ⊙ Save the Children

Dear Reader,

Ten pence seems such a tiny amount doesn't it? Little more than small change and hardly worth bothering about. But in Africa, Asia and Latin America or the Middle East, 10p is enough to help save a child from despairing poverty.

That's why I would like to ask you to support Save the Children with a donation of 10p a day – that's just £3 a month. However small this amount may seem to you, it can make a tremendous difference. And with 1 in 4 of the world's children living in absolute poverty, we urgently need your help.

Ten pence a day is enough to help children caught up in the spread of HIV/AIDS. A virus which is having a devastating effect on the lives of many young people in the developing world.

Ten pence a day can allow Save the Children to respond in emergency situations. Helping us protect children who have lost their homes, families and security to natural disaster, political unrest or the bloody violence of war.

And with £3 a month from you, we can tackle the causes of poverty which force children to work in order to survive.

Please will you help us save more children from poverty by completing the Monthly Bankers Order attached to this letter today?

By doing this you can rescue more youngsters from unimaginable hardship and help give them better and brighter futures.

If you are a UK taxpayer you can make your £3 worth even more at no extra cost to you. Please complete the Gift Aid Declaration which will make every £1 you give worth an extra 28p.

Your monthly gift can safeguard children's rights and give young people a voice in over 70 countries around the world. Your £3 can support our continuing work with children, their families, and communities and help make our influence felt at government level across the world.

There are so many children still living in poverty, so very many young lives we can change for the better. Please will you join Save the Children in partnership by pledging a donation of £3 a month?

Join us in giving children the happy, healthy and secure lives that should be theirs by right.

Thank you.

Yours faithfully

Mike Aaronson.

Director General
Save the Children

Making a start

There are various techniques you can use to make your writing more persuasive and convincing. Broadly, they fall into two categories:

• language
• layout or presentation.

Look at Examples A and B. Example A is a letter which was sent as a mail circular from the charity Save the Children. Example B is a leaflet giving advice to students about meningitis.

The letter contains many language techniques, and its layout also makes an important contribution to the overall message.

• Its **purpose** is to persuade readers to send money to the charity.
• Its **form** is a letter.
• Its **audience** is the selected sample of the public who were sent this mailshot.

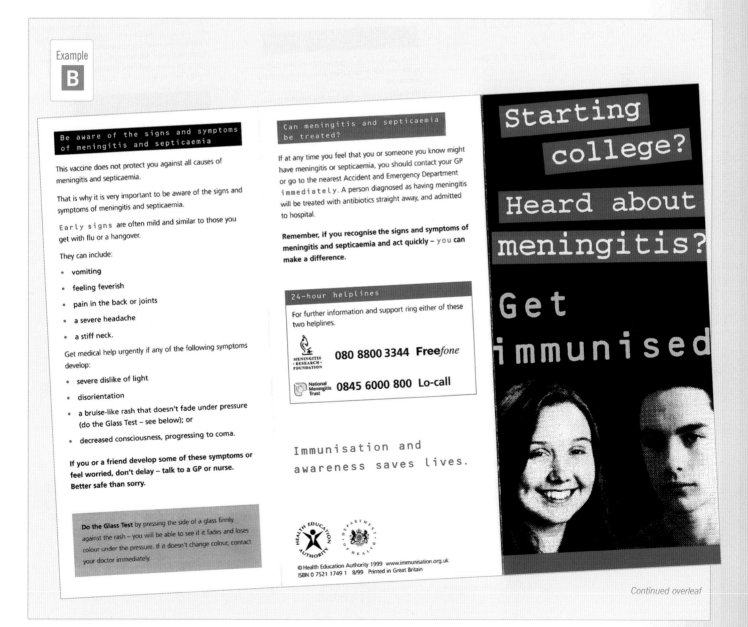

Example **B**

Be aware of the signs and symptoms of meningitis and septicaemia

This vaccine does not protect you against all causes of meningitis and septicaemia.

That is why it is very important to be aware of the signs and symptoms of meningitis and septicaemia.

Early signs are often mild and similar to those you get with flu or a hangover.

They can include:

• vomiting
• feeling feverish
• pain in the back or joints
• a severe headache
• a stiff neck.

Get medical help urgently if any of the following symptoms develop:

• severe dislike of light
• disorientation
• a bruise-like rash that doesn't fade under pressure (do the Glass Test – see below); or
• decreased consciousness, progressing to coma.

If you or a friend develop some of these symptoms or feel worried, don't delay – talk to a GP or nurse. Better safe than sorry.

Do the Glass Test by pressing the side of a glass firmly against the rash – you will be able to see if it fades and loses colour under the pressure. If it doesn't change colour, contact your doctor immediately.

Can meningitis and septicaemia be treated?

If at any time you feel that you or someone you know might have meningitis or septicaemia, you should contact your GP or go to the nearest Accident and Emergency Department immediately. A person diagnosed as having meningitis will be treated with antibiotics straight away, and admitted to hospital.

Remember, if you recognise the signs and symptoms of meningitis and septicaemia and act quickly – you can make a difference.

24-hour helplines

For further information and support ring either of these two helplines.

MENINGITIS RESEARCH FOUNDATION   080 8800 3344 Free*fone*

National Meningitis Trust   0845 6000 800 Lo-call

Immunisation and awareness saves lives.

© Health Education Authority 1999 www.immunisation.org.uk
ISBN 0 7521 1749 1 8/99 Printed in Great Britain

Starting college? Heard about meningitis? Get immunised

Continued overleaf

Example

B

Contd

If you are starting a full-time university or higher education course **you can be immunised against meningococcal infection** which can cause meningitis and septicaemia (also known as blood poisoning). This vaccine protects against one of the most common strains, but does not protect against all strains of the disease. That's why it's important that you know the signs and symptoms of meningitis and septicaemia. If you act quickly, you can make a difference.

Talk to your GP <u>now</u> about having the vaccine <u>before you start</u> university or higher education.

What are meningitis and septicaemia?

Meningitis is an inflammation of the lining of the brain and spinal cord. It is caused by either bacteria or viruses. In septicaemia, bacteria infect the blood and may spread through the body to make you very ill. Meningitis and septicaemia can kill.

How serious are meningitis and septicaemia?

Meningitis and septicaemia are quite rare, but can be extremely dangerous, resulting in deafness, blindness, loss of limbs or even death. However, if symptoms are noticed and treatment is given quickly people can recover fully.

Who is most at risk?

Cases in students occur mostly among first-years. These cases are particularly likely in the first few weeks of starting university or college.

How common is the disease and how is it spread?

Nearly one in four young people naturally carry the bacteria in the nose and throat without developing meningitis or septicaemia.

The bacteria can be spread from one person to another by coughing, sneezing or direct contact such as sharing a glass or kissing. No one knows what triggers the disease.

What is the vaccine?

The vaccine provides protection against group A and C meningitis and septicaemia. The vaccine is not live. It contains parts of the bacteria which should protect you but cannot give you meningitis or septicaemia. You only need one dose.

What protection does the vaccine provide?

One injection should provide protection that lasts for 3 to 5 years. It is important to be immunised as soon as possible but you should remain alert for the signs and symptoms of meningitis and septicaemia.

Where should you go to be immunised?

You should arrange to get the vaccine at your GP surgery. Ring up and make an appointment. Give your GP at least a week's notice to order the vaccine. It is best to get immunised before you go to university or college. If you don't get the chance to visit your GP, then get the vaccine when you start university or college.

Are there any side effects from the vaccine?

Possible side effects of the vaccine are usually mild and short term. About 1–2 days after being immunised you may have a sore arm and some redness and swelling where the injection was given. This will usually go away within a few days. Some people might develop a slight temperature lasting a few hours.

Are there any reasons not to have this vaccine?

You should not have the vaccine if you are ill and running a temperature at the time of the immunisation. If you think you might be pregnant, you should tell your GP.

Activity 1.10a

1 Find the following language features in Example A. You have come across most of them in earlier units.
  a) An informal style producing a familiar, friendly tone (see the use of *we* and *you*).
  b) Use of contrast to bring home a point.
  c) Use of repetition to emphasise the small sacrifice each donor is asked to make.
  d) Direct appeal to the reader through questions.
  e) Use of facts and statistics to add force to the persuasion.
  f) Use of lists to stress the problems facing the world's poor.

2 Some more difficult techniques:
  g) Comment on the use of adjectives. See for example the final sentence of the letter.
  h) The **structure** of a piece of writing is the order in which the points or ideas are presented. How does the structure of this letter contribute towards its overall impact?

3 Look at the layout, or presentation, of Example A. How are colour, font, photographs and design used to enhance the persuasive effect of the letter?

Activity 1.10b Comment on the presentational devices used in the leaflet (Example B).

Serious practice

UNIT ACTIVITY 1.10 Write the *wording* for a leaflet, to be distributed to visitors to your town or area, to advise strangers how to get the most from their visit.

Hints

◆ Adopt the style of an advice leaflet. Look at the information on this page.
◆ Read the question carefully. Identify the words which refer to purpose, form and audience.

COURSEWORK OR EXAMINATION?
Decide beforehand whether you are producing a leaflet for coursework or for examination practice.

◆ If it is for **coursework**, you could use the whole array of presentational devices available in ICT.
◆ If it is for **examination** practice, you should concentrate on the wording and the headings. There would be no marks awarded for visual appearance; marks would be awarded for appropriate style and the overall concept. Nor should you attempt to produce a folded sheet with six panels for examination practice. You could roughly indicate intended layout, but should not waste time actually producing it.

ADVICE LEAFLETS

Language
◆ Most leaflets have a friendly style and tone, addressing the reader as *you*.
◆ They tend to have short sentences so that important information is explained clearly.
◆ Sometimes they are written in a 'question and answer' format, for example, *What can you do on a cold, rainy day? There are plenty of indoor places of interest ....*
◆ Sometimes the language is imperative (see Unit 1.3), for example, *Visit the old gatehouse.*
◆ Sometimes the language has a stronger advisory tone, for example, *You should make a point of visiting the ....*

Structure
◆ In leaflets, the writing is broken up into short, bite-size sections.
◆ Each section normally has a subheading, or a question, which is addressed in the short section of text below it.
◆ There are usually clearly defined sections on the different panels of the leaflet.
◆ Somewhere there will be contact details, or a form, from the organisation which has produced the leaflet.
◆ The front panel has generally very little writing: it is really no more than a title page.

Layout
◆ Most leaflets are A4 sheets with two folds to produce six equal-size panels.
◆ Look at a range of leaflets to see the presentational devices used. You will find:
  – variety of font styles, sizes and colours
  – use of colour to draw attention to key points or headings
  – use of photographs and graphics to break up the print
  – use of bullet points and numbering
  – use of **bold**, *italics* and underlining.

WHAT EXAMINERS ARE LOOKING FOR
The main assessment objective tested in Unit Activity 1.7 is your ability to 'adapt writing for particular purpose and audiences'. You should study the style and layout of leaflets by reading a variety of different types.

Unit 1.11

Effective endings

The unit activity is to write three endings for different purposes (see page 49).

EXTRACT **A**

The animals peep through the window at the pigs and the neighbouring farmers who are squabbling over the dining table:

Twelve voices were shouting in anger, and they were all alike. No question, now, what had happened to the faces of the pigs. The creatures outside looked from pig to man, and from man to pig, and from pig to man again; but already it was impossible to say which was which.

from Animal Farm by George Orwell

EXTRACT **B**

Atticus's daughter, Scout, explains to her father that the monster of their childhood, Boo Radley, is not the drooling ghoul so many of the townsfolk think:

'Atticus when they finally saw him, why he hadn't done any of those things … Atticus he was real nice. …'

His hands were under my chin, pulling up the cover, tucking it around me.

'Most people are, Scout, when you finally see them.'

He turned out the light and went into Jem's room. He would be there all night, and he would be there when Jem waked up in the morning.

from To Kill a Mockingbird by Harper Lee

EXTRACT **C**

And in the middle of them, with filthy body, matted hair, and with unwiped nose, Ralph wept for the end of innocence, the darkness of man's heart, and the fall through the air of the true, wise friend called Piggy.

The officer, surrounded by these noises, was moved and a little embarrassed. He turned away to give them time to pull themselves together; and waited, allowing his eyes to rest on the trim cruiser in the distance.

from Lord of the Flies by William Golding

Making a start

How do I stop this thing?

Finding an effective opening is difficult enough, but ending a piece of writing convincingly is even more difficult. Research has shown that GCSE English students do not know how to finish their essays. This was true at all grades, including grades A and A★.

What's the problem?

Imagine the situation. It is towards the end of a long examination. You have been concentrating for a long time, and the invigilator says 'Five minutes!' Somewhere at the back of your mind a voice is urging you to check your work for punctuation and spelling. You race to say what you have to say. Now you need an ending. In desperation you jot down the first idea you think of.

Is it surprising that so many promising essays finish so badly? This is serious because it is the poor ending which gives the final impression to the examiner of the quality of your writing.

What can you do about it?

If you are writing a piece for coursework, you should try out various endings to find the most effective.

In an examination, if you are armed with some ideas for endings, you should be able to adapt one to suit your task.

Different ways of ending your writing

Here are some final sentences from speeches supporting the proposition: 'Capital punishment is wrong':

1 **Repeat the first sentence**, for example:

   First sentence: *I am strongly opposed to capital punishment.*
   Final sentence: *I hope I have shown you why I am strongly opposed to capital punishment.*

2 **A quotation,** for example:

   Whether you are a Christian or not, there is truth in the Commandment: 'Thou shalt not kill'.

3 **Just stop**, for example:

   Sometimes condemned prisoners live for years on death row.

4 **Add an afterthought**, for example:

   I don't agree with corporal punishment either.

5 **A summary of the views expressed in the essay,** for example:

   So my objections to capital punishment are that the methods used are often barbaric; that it does not reduce crime; that innocent people have been executed.

6 **A rhetorical question,** for example:

   How many of us, I wonder, would be prepared to act as executioner?

7 **A short, powerful statement,** for example:

   All life is sacred.

8 A direct challenge to the reader, using *you*, for example:

So which of you would like the job of explaining to the grieving family that the wrong man has been executed?

9 Present the reader or listener with a stark choice, for example:

So which is better: the barbaric vengeance of execution, or a long prison sentence with the possibility of remorse and rehabilitation?

10 Use a telling statistic or piece of research, for example:

Those so keen to execute murderers on the grounds that capital punishment deters others, should remember one telling fact: the murder rates in states with capital punishment are the same as in those states without.

Note: Research and statistics are common persuasive techniques in coursework essays, but are not often possible in examination answers – unless, of course, you feel confident enough to make up the statistics!

Activity 1.11a

1 With a partner, decide which of the above endings are effective, and which are unsatisfactory. Compare your responses with others in the class.
2 Adopt the opposing point of view and write four of your own final sentences modelled on the most effective ones you identified in Activity 1.11a. In other words, you have to argue in favour of capital punishment.

On page 46 are the endings to three famous novels which you might have read. How effective are they as endings?

Activity 1.11b

If you have read any of the novels from which Extracts A, B and C are taken, think about how far the endings meet this definition of an effective ending:

● It achieves a satisfying close.
● It refers back to earlier themes and events.
● It restates the main theme(s) in a new way.

If you have not read any of them, look at the endings of some books which you have read, and do the same exercise.

The last paragraph

So far we have looked at final sentences only. However, it is better to think of your ending in terms of a last paragraph rather than a single sentence. This allows you to build up to your final statement.

Take the short powerful ending already mentioned, *All life is sacred.* This final sentence might have come at the end of a paragraph like this:

Some crimes are so horrific that it is difficult to regard the criminal as a fellow human being. The newspapers call such people 'beasts' and 'monsters', as if that helps us explain the dreadful things some people do. But I still believe it is wrong to take another life, even if that life is regarded as worthless. All life is sacred.

This shows how effective a short statement can be when summing up an argument. This final paragraph brings the essay to a satisfying close.

Activity 1.11c   Write final paragraphs of about two or three sentences each to build up to these sentences:

a) *How many of us, I wonder, would be prepared to act as executioner?*

b) *So which of you would like the job of explaining to the grieving family that the wrong man has been executed?*

c) *So which is better: the barbaric vengeance of execution, or a long prison sentence with the possibility of remorse and rehabilitation?*

Use the paragraph above as a model.

Serious practice

UNIT ACTIVITY 1.11   Choose three topics from the list below and compose a **final paragraph** for each.

- Aim to write about three to four sentences.
- Give each ending a particular twist, using the list on pages 47–8 as a starting point.
- If you have already written on the topic, look again at the ending you used, and improve it by redrafting.

This activity is best done with essays you have already written in response to earlier units. This list will remind you of topics covered:

- 'It's always wrong to lie' – a speech for a school debate (Unit 1.1)
- The Barnardo's advertisement featuring the baby – a letter to a newspaper supporting or opposing their decision not to print the advertisement (Unit 1.2)
- A report for your class tutor advising on how to improve the classroom environment (Unit 1.3)
- A speech and a letter supporting or opposing the banning of *Big Issue* sellers from local streets (Unit 1.4)
- The class captain's inaugural speech (Unit 1.5)
- A magazine article in response to either Tony Blair's speech about the environment or the letter from the full-time mother and housewife (Unit 1.6)
- An essay about either the benefits and drawbacks of being an only child or the benefits or drawbacks of part-time work for GCSE students (Unit 1.7)
- An article arguing for or against school sports or car ownership (Unit 1.8)
- An essay for or against space exploration (Unit 1.9)

YOUR FINAL PARAGRAPH
If you use a basic structure of four paragraphs, then an argument essay might look like this:

- **Paragraph 1** introduces the topic and expresses a viewpoint.
- **Paragraphs 2 and 3** expand on your reasons for holding that view, bringing in anecdotes, examples and detail.
- **Paragraph 4** rounds off the argument in a satisfying way. It should do more than simply repeat the wording of the opening paragraph. It may not introduce a new argument, but it will restate your view in a convincing new way.

Your aim is to achieve a satisfying close.

WHAT EXAMINERS ARE LOOKING FOR
In judging the overall effectiveness of a piece of writing, examiners look at the ending to see how the topic is rounded off.

Hint

Read the question carefully. Identify the words which refer to purpose, form and audience.

Unit 1.12

Bringing it all together

The unit activity is to practise the range of skills and techniques learned in Units 1.1–1.11 (see page 53).

Making a start

This unit is different from the other units. It gives you practice in writing to argue, persuade and advise using all the tips and techniques you have studied in the previous units.

The unit consists of extracts about problems in the developing world such as famine in Africa, and ways of addressing the problems. It raises moral issues: Should we feel any guilt because we live comfortably? Do we have a responsibility to send aid to distant countries when there are problems on our own doorstep?

Read the extracts and then select at least one task from the unit activity.

EXTRACT A

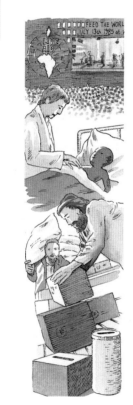

More wealth, less aid

The developed world has never been wealthier, yet levels of overseas aid have been falling. A recent report stated that aid had to double to avert disaster for southern Africa.

Some of the 1.4 billion people worldwide who gathered round their TV sets in 1984 to watch Mick Jagger and the rest wiggling their hips for Live Aid had probably just switched on for the music, but many of them also wanted to have their faith in humanity restored. The horrifying famine in Ethiopia, in which a million people died, should never have been allowed to happen – and pledging a few pounds made everyone feel that the west would never allow it to be repeated.

Eighteen years later, here we are again: shocking pictures of malnourished children, refugees walking miles in search of food, and a stark warning that up to 15 million people are facing starvation across southern Africa. ...

Raising aid budgets means slicing expenditure from somewhere else. Even if there is strong support for greater spending on foreign aid, reallocating it from health, education and the social security budget, is harder to sell.

Oxfam, which spends about half its money in Africa, says the idea that the public have suffered from 'compassion fatigue' is a myth. It received £20m in public donations in 1984/5, £35m in 1995/6, and just under £75m in the last year.

from an article by Heather Stewart, produced by The Guardian in association with Concern

Extract A: Language and meaning

- What is 'compassion fatigue'? This is of great concern to charities. They spend large sums of money on advertising appeals and mailshots, and the worry is that the public become numb to the suffering portrayed. If we are bombarded with images of suffering people, do we begin to shrug and ignore them? This explains why advertisers sometimes turn to more shocking images: see the Barnardo's advertisement in Unit 1.2, for example.
- Note the snappy headline using **antithesis** (opposites).
- The third paragraph is a good example of the use of the colon to introduce a list.

EXTRACT B

WHY SOME CHOCOLATE IS SIMPLY DIVINE

This is a tale of how eating chocolate can help the world. Most people with jobs in the UK rely on knowing, more or less, how much they will earn, so they can plan ahead. Disasters, of course, do happen. People fall ill or lose their jobs – but even then they can qualify for state benefits and support. However bad things are, no one really starves or has to deny their children an education.

Sadly, this is not true for a lot of farmers living in poor countries that have overdue loans from the banks and businesses of wealthier parts of the world. The governments of these 'developing' countries have been so desperate to earn dollars to pay back some of what they owe that they encourage their farmers to grow 'cash crops' for export – crops such as coffee, tea and the cocoa used to make chocolate.

It's an approach that has made millions of farmers dependent on the value of a single crop. Any drop in the price they get for their bananas, coffee or cocoa beans has a huge impact on their fortunes.

In Ghana there are about two million cocoa growers producing, on average, only five bags of beans a year, currently worth just £167 – too little to avoid debt and poverty. Today many crops are being sold for the same price they made in the mid-1980s. ...

Some farmers are more fortunate. This is because they are protected by being members of a co-operative, which offers them a reasonable and stable price for the crop they produce. A good example is the Kuapa Kokoo co-op in Ghana. The co-op insists on decent health and safety controls on its 35,000 cocoa growing members' farms. It has even invested in its own chocolate company ensuring that they get a fair share of the money earned from the sale of their beans abroad. The company produces brands such as Divine and Dubble bars. They are among an increasing number of Fairtrade products available in UK shops. Over the past ten years Fairtrade has developed into a movement involving hundreds of products. Though few of them have the added attraction of Fairtrade chocolate: capable of making you feel greedy and virtuous at the same time.

from an article by Jerome Monahan in
The Guardian, *15 October 2002*

Extract B: Language and meaning

- The headline is a pun, a play on words. This is a common technique to interest a reader, but it is not always possible to think of a pun in an examination!
- Note how the opening sentence intrigues and draws in the reader. This is a good example of how quite complicated subject-matter involving politics and economics can be made interesting and relevant.
- The ending is also effective. Can you explain why?
- This piece appeared in the Education section of the newspaper and was intended to be a learning resource for fourteen-year-olds. Are there any signs that it has been written with that readership in mind?

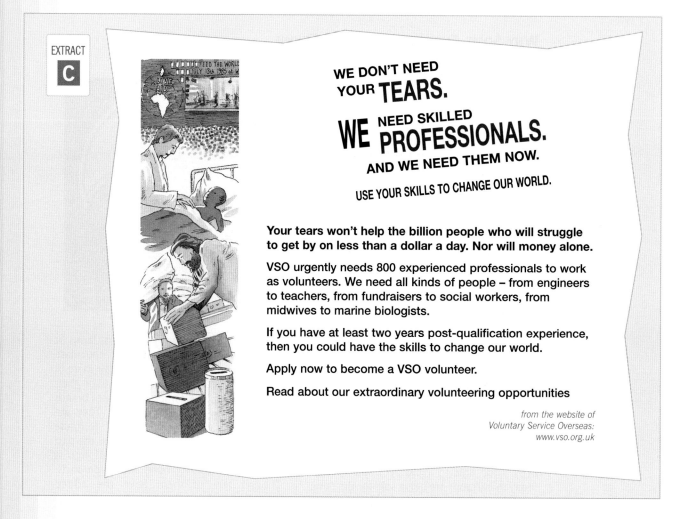

EXTRACT C

WE DON'T NEED YOUR **TEARS.**

WE NEED SKILLED **PROFESSIONALS.**

AND WE NEED THEM NOW.

USE YOUR SKILLS TO CHANGE OUR WORLD.

Your tears won't help the billion people who will struggle to get by on less than a dollar a day. Nor will money alone.

VSO urgently needs 800 experienced professionals to work as volunteers. We need all kinds of people – from engineers to teachers, from fundraisers to social workers, from midwives to marine biologists.

If you have at least two years post-qualification experience, then you could have the skills to change our world.

Apply now to become a VSO volunteer.

Read about our extraordinary volunteering opportunities

from the website of
Voluntary Service Overseas:
www.vso.org.uk

Extract C: Language and meaning

- VSO stands for Voluntary Service Overseas. It has operated for many years sending volunteers with the necessary skills to carefully chosen locations, sometimes to teach, sometimes for a specific project. It differs from most Gap Year organisations in that it is very selective about its volunteers and is looking for skills already acquired in the world of work.
- What are the features of the style and layout which tell you that this is a persuasive piece of advertising? Look back to Unit 1.2 and the *Save the Children* letter in Unit 1.10.

Serious practice

UNIT ACTIVITY 1.12 Choose one or more from this range of tasks. You will have practised the skills required in earlier units.

Extracts A, B and C will give you ideas which you can refer to and draw upon in your writing. You could also do your own research to give your writing a more individual and authoritative feel.

1 Your English teacher is considering taking a year or two out of teaching in the UK to apply as a VSO volunteer in the developing world. Write to your teacher advising him or her whether to apply.

You might consider:
- information from the VSO website
- the skills he or she could bring to the project
- how he or she might gain personally from the experience
- possible drawbacks.

2 Write a speech for a debate entitled: *Foreign aid should be stopped. The money should be used to solve problems in our own country.*

3 Write to your local supermarkets persuading them to stock more Fairtrade products. (There is more information on the Fairtrade movement at www.learn.co.uk)

4 Write a speech to be delivered in an assembly persuading your year group to support a fundraising day to relieve famine in Africa.

You could include:
- research from your reading and other sources
- the benefits for the recipients – and for the givers
- counter-arguments (for example: how much of the money raised would pay for administration and large offices in London?)
- the best approach – small scale? sponsorship of a school or community?

5 Write advising your headteacher on how best to spend a sum of money raised at a school fundraising event.

The options might include:
- sponsoring a child through school (£50–£100 per year)
- a clean water project for a village
- a donation to Oxfam for famine relief
- setting up a Fairtrade co-operative.

WHAT EXAMINERS ARE LOOKING FOR

Examiners prefer to see candidates writing in a lively, individual style rather than playing safe with accurate but dull language choices. As the mark schemes say, effective answers will 'show ambition in and maintain secure control over choices of grammar, punctuation and spelling'.

BEFORE YOU START ...
Here is a checklist to help you approach the task in an organised way:

- **Who is this for?** Think about the audience: their age, values, level of interest in and sympathy for your views. (Unit 1.4)
- Having identified the audience, what **style** would be appropriate? How formal do you need to be? What kind of tone should you adopt? (Unit 1.5)

- What **form** of writing is expected? Have you thought about the style and layout of, for example, a letter, an article or a leaflet? (Unit 1.6)
- Have you **planned** effectively? Have you carried out a brainstorm or produced a mind map? Has this led to a paragraph plan? (Unit 1.7)
- The **opening** is important. Have you considered a range of options? (Unit 1.8)

- As you write the piece, are your **ideas flowing logically** one to the next towards a conclusion? (Unit 1.9)
- Are there some specific **persuasive techniques** you could include, either of language or presentation? (Unit 1.10)
- Finally, can you round off the writing effectively with an **ending** which restates your case in a new way? (Unit 1.11)

Unit 2.1

Writing to inform

The unit activity is to produce the text of a leaflet (see page 57).

SEAT BELTS

One in fifteen children (two in a class of thirty) can expect to be in a road accident before their sixteenth birthday. Wearing properly tested seat belts and restraints saves lives and cuts down the risk of serious injury.

A Transport Research Laboratory survey showed that only 43 per cent of teenagers and adult rear passengers wear seat belts. Over 25 per cent of 5–13-year-olds were unrestrained. An unrestrained child travelling in a car is approximately three times more likely to sustain a head injury than a restrained child.

School transport has been the focus of public concern and action has been taken on this significant aspect of road safety. Regulations introduced in April 1996 require the provision of a seat with a seat belt for at least the number of children carried, a child being defined as between 3 and 15 years of age. A lap belt is the minimum required fitting. The regulation applies to home–school transport, school trips and other trips where the vehicle is hired to transport children.

Small vehicles, i.e. minibuses, are less affected by the regulations. The demand for seat belts on these vehicles is such that the major UK manufacturers now fit lap and diagonal belts as standard on new vehicles.

based on information from Health Evidence Bulletins Wales, Hertfordshire Accident Prevention Group, School Transport News Online

Making a start

Writing to inform is mainly about facts, details, perhaps some statistics and figures. Explaining the implications of the facts and describing the effect of certain actions may come later. Different **forms** of writing give us information, for example, biography, travel writing and brochures, personal reminiscences of places and people. (See Unit 2.6 for more about forms of writing.)

Read Unit Activity 2.1 on page 57 carefully.

Planning your leaflet

Gathering ideas

What you need to be able to do when writing to inform is to put together information from different **sources** into a coherent, full and interesting account. Information comes from various sources:

- other people's knowledge and research which may be found in books, leaflets or on the Internet
- your own knowledge
- your own research of issues or your own experiences of people and places.

The example opposite is an article which presents information on seat belts from a number of sources, with special reference to children. This is your first source for Unit Activity 2.1.

Activity 2.1a	1 List six important pieces of information as they appear in the article.
	2 Put them in order of importance. Number them 1–6, with 1 being the most important and 6 the least important.
	3 What is the **main point** of information being made in the article?
	4 Why do you think you should include the sources of your information? (You will notice that the sources of all extracts taken from published writing are included in this book.)

It is important to have more than one source of information in order to give your writing **credibility**. The article is one source, and another is your proposed audience.

Activity 2.1b	Ask your audience – the students in your school – for information. Here are some questions you could ask them. Add some of your own.

- When did you last ride in a car/school bus/taxi?
- Did anyone tell you to put your seat belt on?
- Do you always do it?
- Do your parents/drivers always wear a seat belt?
- Do you always belt-up in the back seat of the car?
- Does your school transport comply with the regulations in the article?

Remember that it is **facts** you want, not **opinions**. Another source for facts on the topic is from actual, personal experience – yours and that of other people.

---

i KEY WORDS AND PHRASES

leaflet The form of writing chosen for Unit Activity 2.1. The text of a leaflet presents factual information and evidence on the topic. It may make recommendations, but its main purpose is to give information about a subject.

sources The different places from which you can find information. You should name your sources.

main point It is important to be clear about the main point being made. The main point of the article is that children wearing seatbelts is an issue of concern and complexity.

readers Always have in mind the age, interests and situation of your readers. You should always know who you are writing for.

credibility Your sources must be believable and respected. That is why you need more than one and why you should name them. Your material and conclusions should be trustworthy. People might want to check your sources.

facts It is a fact that 'A Transport Research Laboratory survey showed that only 43 per cent of teenagers and adult rear passengers wear seat belts.'

opinions It is an opinion that seat belts should be fitted to all public transport by manufacturers.

topic sentence The sentence which sums up what the paragraph is about. It is not necessarily the first sentence. It could be the last sentence.

Activity 2.1c Carry out this research:

1 What information can you gather from your family about wearing seat belts?
2 Find someone who has been injured or nearly injured when not wearing a seat belt. Ask them for facts about the experience.
3 Find and interview somebody who was probably saved from injury by wearing a belt.
4 When else are seat belts worn? Why?

Paragraph plan

You need to gather all of your material together with full details of your sources and begin to arrange it. The next stage then is to design and plan the first draft of the writing.

Three main sources have been provided here: the article, your proposed audience and personal experience. This suggests that the main body of your writing will have three sections. You also need an introduction and a rounded conclusion. So you have five sections to your writing. Each section could be a paragraph.

Activity 2.1d Work out a paragraph plan for your task in Unit Activity 2.1.

Activity 2.1e Decide what you are going to write in each paragraph. Start by writing a **topic sentence** for each paragraph and then think about what else you want to write. Do not worry about style at this point – just get some words down.

> **Hint** Your paragraph plan might look like this:
>
> - **Paragraph 1: Introduction**
>   Show that you understand the question. Indicate what you are going to deal with and the sources you will use.
> - **Paragraph 2: Main points from the article**
>   You need the facts and figures but try to use your own words.
> - **Paragraph 3: Main points from interviews with students**
>   Quote some of the answers directly for effect. Report some of the others. Summarise the responses.
> - **Paragraph 4: Main points from personal experience interviews**
>   Some of these might be very dramatic. Emphasise that these are facts, reality, information about what really happened.
> - **Paragraph 5: Conclusion**
>   You need to remind your readers about the factual requirements – the regulations concerning seat belts. You do not need to make a persuasive, emotional point – that is not asked for. *Let the facts speak for themselves.*

> **Hint** You could draw large circles in which to do this.
> For example for Paragraph 3 of the plan above, you might write:
>
> The topic sentence is underlined.
>
> *Both at home and school, children remain at risk because seat belt laws and regulations are being ignored. Our survey amongst students in this school showed that ....*

Style and structure

When you have written a first draft and are happy with the content of your leaflet, you need to improve the writing style, organisation of ideas and technical skills. Look at the information opposite.

Serious practice

Now that you have planned your writing, complete the unit activity.

UNIT ACTIVITY 2.1 There is to be a Road Safety Awareness Week at your school.
Using the material you have collected from a number of sources, write the *text* of a leaflet, to be distributed to students and parents, which informs them about the issue of 'Children and seat belts'.

Hints

- Read the question carefully. Identify the words which refer to the topic, your sources, the context, the audience, the form, the purpose.
- Use the information you have gathered already in this unit.
- Whichever **form** of writing you choose or are asked to present, you must write in standard English and in well-structured continuous prose. The question asks for the text of a leaflet. Do not include graphics.
- Are there any words or phrases you should explain to your readers?

FEATURES OF STYLE
Consider using some of these features in your writing:

- *interesting, arresting words* and *phrases* – there is no reason why information cannot be vivid, dramatic and engaging
- rhetorical questions, lists, emphasis, a commanding voice
- signpost words to separate points, such as *however, in spite of, it is necessary that* ....
- structural features – see below
- clearly organised ideas, information and evidence
- accurate spelling and punctuation
- a good, eye-catching and engaging title.

STRUCTURAL FEATURES

An engaging title
This may be humorous, witty or clever – a pun is good, but make sure it's appropriate and in good taste. The title should be short.

Varied length of paragraph
In paragraph 4 of your plan, a really dramatic account of a personal experience might be split into two paragraphs for effect, however brief, for example, 'If only I'd been wearing my seat belt, I would not have gone through the windscreen', Sarah told me.

Varied length of sentence
Short sentences can be arresting, emphatic and effective.

Indentation
This gives shape to your leaflet.

Bullet points
These can be used to present a lot of factual information concisely.

Headings
Introduce the topic of the section or paragraph and catch the reader's eye.

Subheadings
Allow you to direct your readers' thoughts.

Do not overdo these features. They should support your continuous writing, not replace it. You get marks for what you *write* in relation to the Assessment Objectives, not for being a graphic genius.

WHAT EXAMINERS ARE LOOKING FOR
In the exam:

- at grade C: 'more selection of information for interest'; 'information likely to cover a range of aspects'
- at grade A: 'wide range of interesting information'; 'growing subtlety of purpose (to inform) and ability to manipulate reader'

In coursework:

- at grade C: 'inform through a structured, well expressed piece of continuous prose'
- at grade A: 'demonstrate a variety of registers and styles in informative writing'.

Unit 2.2

Writing to explain

The unit activity is to write an account (see page 61).

Looking after your horse

There are a number of reasons for grooming your horse properly. Grooming cleans the horse's skin and tones the muscles. The horse's blood circulation is improved and the coat will have a healthy and enhanced appearance.

A good bristle brush is used for grooming, strongly applied. Strength and weight are needed. It is best to stand away from the horse and lean your weight onto the brush. This will penetrate the coat more effectively. Horses enjoy grooming so groom three or four times a week for forty-minute sessions.

When properly groomed, your horse will look better, feel better and be healthier.

adapted from Horses and Stables *by Sir F. Fitzwygram*

Making a start

There are a number of different ways of explaining, including:

- how things work
- how to do something
- the reasons for things happening
- what you believe or how you feel about something.

Writing which explains can be found everywhere: novels, non-fiction, media, biography, recipe books, instruction manuals, travel writing, personal reflective writing, and in many other forms.

When you write to explain, you need to make the details of the subject-matter clear. That is, you need to make the subject intelligible and plain to the reader. To do this, you have to make precise connections between ideas, events or actions.

The example above is a piece of continuous prose writing which explains some reasons for grooming a horse and how to do it.

Activity 2.2a   Read the extract carefully.
1   What is the connection between the title and the content?
2   Comment on the paragraph structure – how is the content structured?
3   Using key words and a list of bullet points, explain:
   a)   why you should groom a horse
   b)   how you should do it.

Linking cause and effect

One of the aspects of explaining something is to make connections between *cause* and *effect*.

Activity 2.2b   The writer of the extract implies that there are a number of effects which result from doing certain things. Explain what this means by completing the table.

Cause	Effect
Grooming a horse properly	
	More effective penetration of the horse's coat
Grooming three or four times each week	

Clarifying the points

Another aspect of explaining is to provide enough detail for your audience in order to clarify the points you are making.

Look back to question 3 of Activity 2.2a – the extract gives *eight* reasons why you should groom a horse and explains *five* of ways of doing it.

Read Unit Activity 2.2 on page 61 carefully.

Planning your explanation

Gathering ideas

Activity 2.2c   Working in pairs or small groups, brainstorm some ideas for Unit Activity 2.2. Remember that there are two aspects to the writing – cycling and camping.

KEY TERMS

Sources
Brainstorm ideas in a group – you will get more ideas from different experiences and perspectives this way.

Illustrations
Decide at the planning stage if you are going to use any illustrative material to enhance your writing. You might want to illustrate your account with a map which explains where you are planning to go.

Facts and opinions
Since your main purpose is to explain a sequence of related events or ideas, your writing will have more fact than opinion. But you can also explain your feelings about the topic in a vivid way.

Credibility
Make sure your plans and explanations are viable and possible. Readers will want to believe and engage with your writing

Hints

- Explain the preparations you need to make in advance of the trip.
- Explain who is to be responsible for what amongst the three of you.
- Detail the planning required.
- Explain where you are going – your itinerary.
- Explain what you need to ensure your cycle and equipment is up to scratch.
- Explain what you need for the journey.
- Explain what is good about cycling in the countryside.
- Detail what you need for a weekend camping.
- Explain the positive aspects of camping.
- Explain the benefits of the weekend.

Paragraph plan

Having gathered material from your sources, you need to explain the precise *connections* between your ideas with clarity and the appropriate degree of formality.

Activity 2.2d Organise and sequence your brainstorm ideas into paragraphs.

FORM

The form of writing required in the unit activity is an **account**. You can give an account of what you intend to do as well as of something you have done.

You should write in well-organised, continuous prose using paragraphs. You may also include lists, bullet points, diagrams and tables, if appropriate. Anything which helps to explain what you are doing is useful.

But remember:

◆ This is a *writing* activity so use standard English and an extended vocabulary where you can.

◆ Your writing should be stylish and engaging. It should not be functional and mechanical, stripped of interesting words and phrases.

REGISTER

The register should be **formal**. Your readers will be intelligent people of your own age. Formal means it should be appropriate for publication, using standard English sentences and paragraphs. You should be aware of your audience but not be over-familiar.

Slang, 'street', words and colloquialism are not appropriate. Dialogue is probably inappropriate for this task too. However, dialect words and technical words will probably be a feature.

Activity 2.2e Plan what you are going to write in each paragraph. Start by writing a **topic sentence** for each paragraph and then think about what else you want to write.

Hint

Your plan might look something like this:

◆ **Paragraph 1: Introduction**
Show that you understand the question. Emphasise the purpose – to explain.
Show you understand who your readers are.

◆ **Paragraph 2: Explain the preparations for the trip**
Use material from the brainstorm. Include detail and an explanation of reasons and feelings for doing things.

◆ **Paragraph 3: Explain the requirements for camping**
Link cause and effect. Explain feelings as well as details.

◆ **Paragraph 4: Conclusion**
Explain the purpose and benefits of the weekend in a general way as in the brief last paragraph of the extract on page 58.

Hint

You could draw large circles in which to do this.

For example for Paragraph 2 of the plan above, you might write:

> *Preparation for the journey must include planning the route with the help of an OS map, organising provisions, working out timings and making sure you can safely carry everything you need.*

You can move on from here to provide the detail your explanation needs. It might be best to put the topic sentence first for an explaining task.

Style

Remind your readers (one of whom will be grading your work) that your **purpose** is to explain. You can explain feelings and experiences as well as details in a vivid way, for example:

> *It's not difficult to explain to a camper, the thrilling sense of freedom which courses through aching limbs, whilst squatting over an open fire in the tranquil silence of evening as the aroma of supper wafts towards a red- empty sky.*

Serious practice

Now you have planned your explanation, complete the unit activity.

UNIT ACTIVITY 2.2 Your class has been asked to write something for the school magazine which is to feature 'Things to do at the weekend'.

You have decided to write an account which explains how to organise a cycling and camping weekend for a group of three. This could be an account of something you have done in the past or intend to do in the future.

Hint

Read the question carefully. Identify the words which relate to the topic, the audience, the form and the purpose.

 STRUCTURAL FEATURES

Title

An engaging title is needed which you should write last. It should be short, appropriate and sum up what follows.

Sentence length

Vary the length of sentences for effect. Short sentences can be effective even if they are strictly –- but deliberately – ungrammatical, for example: *Why do I like camping? Exhilaration. Independence. Freedom.*

Subheadings, bullet points, indentation

You may want to use these features but they should add something to the writing, not replace continuous prose.

Unit 2.3

Writing to describe

The unit activity is to write a descriptive account or report (see page 65).

The Whispering Land

We set off for the south in the pearly grey dawn light of what promised to be a perfect day. The streets were empty and echoing, and the dew drenched parks and squares had their edges frothed with piles of fallen blooms from the jacaranda trees, heaps of glittering flowers in blue, yellow and pink.

For two days we sped through the typical landscape of the pampa, flat golden grassland in which the cattle grazed knee-deep; occasional clumps of eucalyptus trees, with their bleached and peeling trunks like leprous limbs; small neat estancias, gleaming white in the shade of huge ombu trees that stood massively and grimly on their enormous squat trunks.

In places, the neat fences that lined the road were almost obliterated under a thick cloak of convolvulus, hung with electric blue flowers the size of saucers, and every third or fourth post would have balanced upon it the strange, football-like nest of an oven bird. It was a lush, prosperous and well-fed looking landscape.

from The Whispering Land *by Gerald Durrell*

Making a start

When you write to describe, you should aim to make **telling use** of descriptive **detail**. Almost everything you do or see is capable of being described: people, places, ideas, events, thoughts and feelings, relationships, experiences.

Descriptive writing can be found in fictional writing, biographical writing, eye-witness reports, travel writing, sports reporting, accounts of major events – disasters, celebrations – and in many other forms of writing. The example above is from travel writing, and gives information as well as description.

Activity 2.3a   Read the extract carefully.
1   For each paragraph note the bare facts – the information. Retain the
     person and tense but use your own words. The first paragraph is done for
     you:

Paragraph	What you learn/facts
1	We were heading south. It was dawn. The streets were empty. On the edges of the parks and squares there were fallen jacaranda blooms.
2	
3	

2   Put the bare facts together in a couple of paragraphs. You will need to add
     connectives and rearrange phrases to make good continuous prose.

When you read your own writing, you will see that you have described the
experience (what you were doing) in basic terms. You have also given
information and explanation of where you were and what it looked like. Gerald
Durrell has done this too – but he has done more.

Activity 2.3b   1   Look at these phrases used by Gerald Durrell in the first paragraph:

- *in the pearly grey dawn light*
- *empty and echoing*
- *the dew drenched*
- *frothed with piles*
- *heaps of glittering flowers in blue, yellow and pink.*

Write a sentence or two which explains what is added to the bare facts by
this detailed description. Explain why this is good, **effective writing**.
2   Find two or three examples of **vivid** descriptive writing from each of the
     remaining paragraphs of the extract.
3   Discuss with a partner or group why the detailed descriptive writing is
     engaging and effective.

You have seen how descriptive writing can add detail, understanding and more
information to discursive writing. The vivid embellishment of Durrell's writing
is no self-indulgence. You know *more* about an empty street if it is described as
echoing and *more* about flower blossoms if you know what colour they are.

Read Unit Activity 2.3 on page 65 carefully.

Planning your writing

Gathering ideas

The form of writing requested in the unit activity is a **report** or **account** for a
travel magazine. You need first to decide on a place, or an experience which
includes a place, which you are going to describe. This may be somewhere
unfamiliar or familiar – perhaps somewhere on holiday or a local place.

Hints

- Where is the place?
- What is the setting?
- What is the time of day?
- What aspects of the place do you want to report/ record?
- What extra features are worth mentioning?
- For what is the place famous?
- Find some unusual things to describe.
- Remember that your description will add information and understanding to the place

Hint

Your plan might look like this:

- **Paragraph 1: Introduction**
  Show that you understand the question. Create a title for the article/report. Show that you understand who your readers are and address them appropriately.
- **Paragraph 2: Describe where your place is**
  Give a brief context of how and why you were there. This is equivalent to Durrell's first paragraph.
- **Paragraph 3: Develop your description**
  Focus on one or two particular aspects. Remember detail, added information, coherence through description.
- **Paragraph 4: Conclusion**
  Conclude in a rounded way. Bring your readers back in, recommend a visit, explain why they would benefit.

Activity 2.3c   Brainstorm some ideas about the place you choose to describe for Unit Activity 2.3, with some bare facts – basic descriptions as in Activity 2.3a.

KEY WORDS
Make sure you understand these words and phrases.

telling use
The descriptive words used should not be wasted. Do not use unnecessary embellishment, even if they are vivid and use imagery. Make the words count.

detail
The more you write about a place, experience or event, the more information you are providing.

person and tense
Durrell uses the third person (*we*) and past tense (*were*). This indicates personal, first-hand experience. First or third person writing is stronger than second person writing, especially if you are recounting a personal experience.

connectives
The obvious connectives are *and*, *so*, *then*, but *later*, *very soon*, *in the distance*, *beyond*, *we could see far off* might also work.

vivid, engaging, effective writing
Vivid writing paints a detailed picture demanding the use of the reader's senses. This in turn engages the reader- makes him want to read on, feel a part of the scene, be involved in the experience being described. Effective writing, literally affects the reader, making him changed, moved, interested, altered by the writing.

Paragraph plan

You need to organise your ideas from the brainstorm into a coherent form. Remember some of the important elements which an examiner will be looking for – your work needs to:

- be organised
- communicate clearly
- be coherent.

These are key terms used by examiners.

Activity 2.3d   Organise your ideas in a paragraph plan.

FACT, OPINION AND IMAGINATION
You are writing *discursively*. This means 'proceeding by reasoning, not intuitively'. You are not making this up.

If you read the Durrell extract again, you will see that he has not actually expressed opinions about the 'landscape of the pampa', he has provided the reader with facts – you showed this in Activity 2.3a.

He has done so in an imaginative way. But this does not mean he has made it up. It *does* mean that he has used descriptive words to give the reader a vivid image of what the place was actually like.

The power of vocabulary

When writing to describe, you need to focus particularly on the power of vocabulary. This relates to the Assessment Criteria for exam and coursework for writing to inform, explain and describe which states 'begin to show an extended and developed vocabulary', for the mark range which includes C grade.

The challenge is to use vivid descriptive words but not to overdo it. You need to recall images in your mind. But remember that this is non-fiction writing. The report has to be real as well as engaging and compelling.

For Unit Activity 2.3, therefore, you need to compile a word bank of descriptive words to give the reader a vivid image of what the place is like.

Activity 2.3e   Using your five senses, find words and phrases to describe one of the following settings:

- a city centre
- a barren landscape
- a tropical forest
- a windswept English sea-shore in winter
- a snowy mountainous region
- a derelict, rundown townscape
- a paradise island.

Create words banks for each section of your writing at the planning stage. You can use a thesaurus. But do not over-do descriptive writing. It is your writing and must sound real and authentic.

Serious practice

Now you have planned your description, complete the unit activity.

UNIT ACTIVITY 2.3   You have been asked to contribute an article to *Young Traveller*, a travel magazine for young people. Write a report which describes your experience of visiting an interesting, unusual or memorable place.

FORMS OF WRITING

Writing to describe can take a number of forms. Memos, minutes, plans and summaries – which are some of forms of writing mentioned in the National Curriculum for this triplet – may require succinct and sparing expression. However, an **account** or **report** of an experience and a **record** of an event may be expressed in an elaborate and developed way which shows an extended or developed vocabulary.

WRITING IN A VIVID AND INTERESTING WAY

The National Curriculum also states that, for in writing to inform, explain and describe, you should 'use formal and impersonal language and concise expression'. This does not mean, however, that your vocabulary should be mundane, your ideas poor and your expression limited.

The extract from Gerald Durrell's book is a non-fiction account of part of a journey he made when in Patagonia. He has not imagined what he saw and felt, he has reported it. It is vividly written with an extended vocabulary because he is a stylish writer and the report of his experience benefits from this.

Hint

Here is some descriptive vocabulary for a snowy mountainous region:

arctic	hazy
arid	iron-cold
barren	misty
biting	piercing
bitter	polar raw
blue-grey	precipitous
boulder-strewn	rugged
clear	silent
cold	sun-glinting
craggy	tear-making
deserted	tumbling
desolate	vapid
echoing	weak yellow
empty	wind-whistling
glacial	

Hints

- Read the question carefully. Identify the words which refer to your audience, the form , the purpose and any hints about the content of the writing.
- You may imitate Durrell's third person and past tense.

Unit 2.4

Establishing a relationship with your reader

The unit activity is to write a leaflet to inform and describe (see page 69).

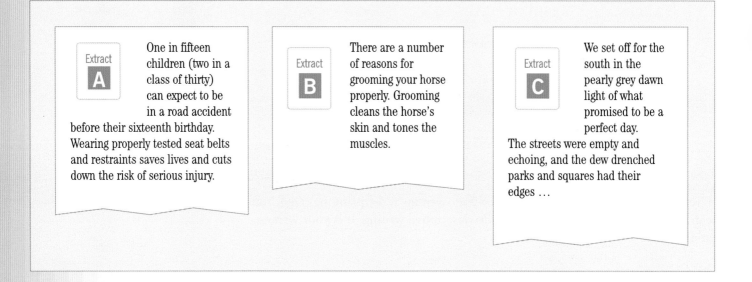

Extract A

One in fifteen children (two in a class of thirty) can expect to be in a road accident before their sixteenth birthday. Wearing properly tested seat belts and restraints saves lives and cuts down the risk of serious injury.

Extract B

There are a number of reasons for grooming your horse properly. Grooming cleans the horse's skin and tones the muscles.

Extract C

We set off for the south in the pearly grey dawn light of what promised to be a perfect day. The streets were empty and echoing, and the dew drenched parks and squares had their edges …

Making a start

Who is your reader?

You should be clear who you are writing for. This will often be stated in the wording of the question, with phrases such as:

- *Write an article to be read by students of your own age*
- *Write to the editor of a newspaper*
- *Inform your local council about the problem of …*
- *Write a speech to be given to a meeting.*

If there is no audience specified in the question, you should imply one in your answer or assume that the reader is the examiner.

Activity 2.4a

1 Look at Extracts A, B and C. These are the opening paragraphs of extracts you have considered in previous units. Who is the audience in each case? Just by reading, focusing and thinking about what was in the writer's mind when composing them, you can see that the audience is different for each.

2 Write one or two sentences for each opening which shows that you understand the audience at whom the writing is targeted.

3 How is the audience linked to the topic? Come back to check this after doing Activity 2.4b

QUESTIONS WITH COMBINED PURPOSES

In Units 2.1–2.3 you thought about and practised writing to inform, explain and describe. You may be set a coursework assignment or exam question which focuses on one element alone as the practice questions did in these units. Or they may be combined. Here are two examples of questions which combine more than one purpose for writing:

◆ You and your family are keen ramblers. **Explain** why you think rambling is a worthwhile pass time and **describe** vividly some of the places you have been.

◆ You are interested in UFOs but lots of people you know are non-believers. Write an account which gives **information** about the evidence for UFOs and **explains** why you believe in them.

Make up a question of your own, on a topic which interests you, which has all three purposes – to inform, explain and describe.

Extract D

Dear Mrs Smith

Welcome to the wonderful world of Scotts of Stow. As somebody who enjoys the convenience of Home Shopping, I'm sure you've come across our catalogues before. I know we haven't tempted you to place an order yet but I am so keen for you to enjoy the benefits of shopping with us ....

from Scotts of Stow catalogue

Extract E

Remember what those boots are made for?

What better way to shift those festive pounds than a long walk? I've been known to stride out in the dark after a huge dinner at Christmas, but these top ten walks are great for day or weekend trips ...

from The Independent Review, 26 December 2002

Extract F

OXFAM REPORTS
Winter 2002
The children on the cover have been forced by drought to leave their home in Afghanistan and to live in temporary camps in Pakistan. But their needs are the same as those young people in Kenya, India and all over the world ... Help Oxfam every time you use your credit card ...

from Oxfam, December 2002

Extract G

Young Reds
The Young Reds end-of-season disco is always well attended by members of the City first team. They come to see which of their number has been voted Player of the Season by the young supporters. But of course you cannot be there if you have not got your ticket ...

from Red and White, Bristol City FC Programme 1998

What do you need to know about your reader?

There are a number of things to consider when thinking about your audience:

- What is or is not the intended age range?
- Is the audience specific?
- What is the level of language ability assumed?
- How does style fit the audience
- How specialised is the audience?
- Is the audience in a particular context?

Activity 2.4b   Read Extracts D, E, F and G. Answer the questions listed above for each one.

KEY WORDS AND PHRASES

audience and readership
These terms are inter-changeable and you will come across both. Writers and editors, especially of magazines, pamphlets. leaflets, media and other informative literature, often refer to the **target audience**, which means the people who will read the writing they produce.

range of readership
Sometimes a piece of writing is targeted at a particular age range which is quite narrow or specific, sometimes at a wide age range and sometimes the age range is not relevant. There are examples of each in Activity 2.4b.

level of language ability assumed
Writing which is technical, describing or explaining a scientific phenomena such as the human genome, would require a level of language ability or vocabulary greater than usual. Some descriptive writing which is not technical also requires this.

specific audience and style
The tone or style of Extracts D, E, F and G varies. Some are detached, while others try to be friendly, almost intimate – they have different people and purposes in mind.

context
Are the audience, for example, in a hall listening to a debate or are they sitting at home?

Read Unit Activity 2.4 on page 69 carefully.

Planning your leaflet

Gathering ideas

Activity 2.4c   Brainstorm some ideas for Unit Activity 2.4.

Hints   Here is some material which you can use to brainstorm. Some of it is from an Oxfam leaflet:

- Nairobi's shanty towns are home to more than 530,000 people.
- The settlements, like Kibera, are extremely poor.
- There is a lack of school places for the children.
- Most primary school children are not at school.

- School buildings are derelict.
- Halima Abdi has lived in Kibera for 25 years. 'I don't even know my ABC' she says.
- 'I want my children to have a chance,' she says.
- Health, hygiene and clean water are also a problem for Halima and her family.
- With money Oxfam can help overcome such problems and provide solutions..

Paragraph plan

Activity 2.4d   Plan your leaflet keeping your young audience in mind.

Hints   Your plan might look like this:

- **Section 1: Introduction**
  Bring your readers in with a good introduction.
- **Section 2: The plight of the children**
  Use material from the brainstorm. Organise it so that it is most effective.

- **Section 3: How readers how can help**
  Think of ways that a Year 6 class might raise money.
- **Section 4: Conclusion**
  Make connections between the parts of your leaflet and the task.

Activity 2.4e   In pairs or groups, experiment with shapes and sizes for your leaflets. They will probably be equivalent to two sides of writing.

- You could include pictures/graphic work.
- Remember that you need to grab the attention of your Year 6 audience immediately. How?

Rhetoric

The **rhetorical question** can be very effective if it is properly used. But you will lose marks if you use it too much.

Children use the rhetorical question frequently, for example:

• *How would you like it if …?*
• *I suppose you think that's funny?*
• *Where would I find another friend like you?*

Another form of rhetoric is statements such as:

• *School? I wouldn't be anywhere else.*
• *If I was any happier I'd die.*

The use of rhetoric can be effective in attracting in your readers' attention and holding it. But make sure it is appropriate.

Serious practice

Now you have planned your leaflet, complete the unit activity.

UNIT ACTIVITY 2.4   Year 6 of a local primary school is having a 'Children like us' week with lots of activities and awareness exercises. Your task is to write a leaflet which:
• *describes* the plight of some children in a Nairobi shanty town
• *informs* your readership what they can do to help.

Hints

◆ Read the question carefully. Identify the words which refer to your audience.

◆ You are obviously concerned with the quality of your writing but what is most important is to show and keep in mind awareness of audience as well as purpose. Ask yourself the questions listed on page 67.

STRUCTURAL FEATURES
You need to write in continuous prose because you will be doing this, essentially, as an English task. However, remind yourself of the structural features mentioned in earlier units:

◆ varied length of paragraphs
◆ varied length of sentences
◆ indentation
◆ quotation which stands out
◆ different use of letter, words, font size
◆ headings and subheadings.

The title
One way of getting the attention of your reader is by having an arresting, hard-hitting title. You are dealing with a serious subject with this task — and with children — so you need to choose a title which:

◆ touches your audience
◆ sums up the subject-matter of your writing.

Unit 2.5

Choosing the right style

The unit activity is to write a contribution to a discussion (see page 73).

Extract **A**

One in fifteen children (two in a class of thirty) can expect to be in a road accident before their sixteenth birthday. Wearing properly tested seat belts and restraints saves lives and cuts down the risk of serious injury.

Extract **B**

There are a number of reasons for grooming your horse properly. Grooming cleans the horse's skin and tones the muscles.

Extract **C**

We set off for the south in the pearly grey dawn light of what promised to be a perfect day. The streets were empty and echoing, and the dew drenched parks and squares had their edges …

KEY TERMS

diction

This refers to the actual words used – the *choice of words and phrases used in speech and writing*. The words *language* and *vocabulary* refer to the same thing.

Examiners refer to 'use of language for effect' or to 'extended and developed vocabulary', all of which is known as diction.(See also page 73.)

syntax

This means sentence construction; the arrangement of words in speech or writing. Sentences may be simple, complex, compound; long or short, even one word for deliberate effect.

Look at the difference in effect between Jane Austen's and Ernest Hemingway's opening sentences (Extracts D and E).

Making a start

Style can be defined as:

> *any specific and deliberate way of using language which characterises a genre, register, purpose or intention in writing.*

The features which create the style of the writing include: **diction**, **syntax**, imagery, rhythm, linguistic and structural features.

The words most often used by students to describe style are *formal* and *informal*. These, on their own, are unhelpful. Try to get away from using these words. Use the terms from this unit instead.

- Sometimes style is defined in terms of *the way in which a certain profession writes*, for example, journalistic style means using the features noted above in the way a journalist does; legalistic style is the way lawyers use language.
- Sometimes style is defined in terms of *who uses it*. For example, you might deliberately write to describe in the style of Ernest Hemingway or write to explain in the style of Jane Austen.
- Sometimes style is defined by a *period of writing*, so you may hear people speak of romantic, classical, modern or post-modern style.

Tone and mood

When people say that the writer has a formal style, they are more accurately referring to the **tone** which has been adopted. The tone of a piece of writing includes its level of formality, detachment or objectivity, irony, bias, commitment, sentimentality, pomposity … and almost limitless other descriptive words.

You need to practise identifying and analysing the tone and style in writing. If you can see the difference in other people's writing, your own style will be more focused and deliberate. Look at the extracts on page 70, which you have seen before. Just by reading them, and remembering their different audiences from Unit 2.4, you can see that they each have a different style and tone.

| Activity 2.5a | Write down your thoughts about the style and tone of Extracts A, B and C, using some of the words on this page as a guide. |

What decides a particular style?

You, as the writer, decide which style to write in, but your choice is affected by:

- the **form** of the writing
- your **audience**
- the **purpose** of the writing.

FORM
The form of your writing might be: an article, a letter, an account, a report, a speech, a leaflet, a pamphlet, an essay, a fictional story, a poem, a biography or a news story, for example.

AUDIENCE
Your readership or audience might be: an adult audience, a friend, young people, a wide readership, specialists such as travellers, or interest groups related to specified topics such as science, society, places and people.

PURPOSE
The purpose with which these units is concerned is to inform, explain and describe.

Activity 2.5b

1 Make a copy of the table below. Complete the table: identify the words in the list which you think apply to Extracts A, B and C. (You might do this as a paired activity.)

| | Extract | | |
Word	A	B	C

bleak	exciting	ironic	sinister
cold	exotic	light-hearted	solemn
committed	explanatory	objective	subjective
cynical	factual	patronising	tearful
descriptive	flippant	reflective	threatening
detached	horrific	respectful	verbose
dismissive	humorous	satirical	vivid
economical	informative	sentimental	warm
emotional	intimate	serious	

2 How do the words you identified in the table compare to your answer to Activity 2.5a?

3 Add more words to the table if appropriate.

Activity 2.5c   What is the style and tone of Extracts D, E and F (page 72)? Read each one carefully then answer the questions.

1 Work in pairs or small groups and discuss:
   a) the tone of each extract using the table for Activity 2.5b
   b) the form, audience and purpose of each extract
   c) the diction of each piece of writing
   d) the length of sentences, noting any variation between the pieces.

2 Write an essay which explains and describes the differences in style used by the three writers

Extract **D**

This is part of a letter written by Jane Austen to her sister in 1801 informing and explaining part of her journey:

Between Luggershall and Everley we made our grand meal, and then with admiring astonishment perceived in what a magnificent manner our support had been provided for. We could not with the utmost exertion consume above the twentieth part of the beef. The cucumber will, I believe, be a very acceptable present, as my uncle talks of having inquired the price of one lately, when he was told a shilling.

from www.pemberley.com/janeinfo

Extract **E**

Here is a descriptive opening of a biographical novel:

Then there was the bad weather. It would come in one day when the fall was over. We would have to shut the windows in the night against the rain and the cold wind would strip the leaves from the trees in the place Contrescarpe.

from A Moveable Feast by Ernest Hemingway

Extract **F**

This is some informative and explanatory writing:

Although none of the great peaks of Snowdonia lies within the boundaries of the forest park, all of them stand close to its borders, and dominate the scenery of the surrounding country. Their summits are within tramping distance of most of the park centres, whilst there are numerous interesting walks from one valley to another across their foothills.

from Snowdonia by H.L. Edlin

Read Unit Activity 2.5 on page 73 carefully.

Planning your writing

Gathering ideas and planning the paragraphs

Activity 2.5d 1 Brainstorm some ideas for Unit Activity 2.5 (see the Hints below).
 2 Organise your ideas in a paragraph plan.

Hints Here is some material to help with your brainstorming.

- Vivisection is defined as *dissection or other painful treatment of living animals for purposes of scientific research.*
- Antibiotics, anaesthetics, vaccines, insulin for diabetes, open heart surgery, kidney dialysis and transplants, treatments for asthma, leukaemia and high blood pressure are just some of the major medical advances that have depended on the use of animals in medical research and testing.
- One anti-vivisection website (www.shac.net/HLS/exposed/kite.html) records the following: 'Clinical reports recorded "rats having fits after dosing for up to one minute" and "cages 85, 95 and 100 had large amounts of dark red blood on their trays". The animal's condition was recorded as "gross and ill with greasy wet fur standing on end". One technician described the animals in this room as "rotting but still alive".'
- It is a concern that animals are suffering, not for real medical science, but for the manufacture of cosmetics and 'life style' drugs.
- Transplantation of animal organs, especially from pigs, is saving lives, including the lives of children.

Tone

What sort of tone do you want to adopt for the unit activity? Look again at the table of tone words in Activity 2.5b. To be effective, you may decide to take a biased stance, so you would need to practise developing a style and tone which is deliberate, obvious and effective. Certainly, the subject-matter does not lend itself to a *light-hearted, humorous* or *flippant* tone. If you feel strongly, the tone might be *angry, inflammatory* and *grave*.

Activity 2.5e

1 Using the table in Activity 2.5b, tick the words which you would expect a reader to use to describe the tone of your speech.

2 Now look again at Extracts A–F in this unit which you considered for their style. What can you learn from them?
   a) Which one comes closest to the approach which suits your topic?
   b) Why might you discount some immediately? (It will be to do with their tone and diction.)

You will need to build word banks as you brainstorm and plan your writing. Think about what would affect you – what would make you respond in, say, an emotional or angry way.

Notice the use made of varied sentence lengths in the writing you have studied. Experiment with length of sentence and syntax.

---

i

THINKING ABOUT DICTION

Diction means the same as:

♦ language
♦ vocabulary.

When you have decided on the style and tone of your writing, you will need the vocabulary to drive it home. For example, if you intend to be emotional and sentimental, you will need appropriate words and phrases, such as:

♦ *poor, helpless animals*
♦ *somebody's pet*

♦ *painful and neglected*
♦ *defenceless, vulnerable*
♦ *unfair*
♦ *selfish*
♦ *frightened and crying.*

At a different point in your writing, when you want to get across the horror of the subject, words such as *blood, vomit. screaming and whimpering, blind, maddened with fear,* might be appropriate.

Serious practice

Now you have planned your writing, complete the unit activity.

UNIT ACTIVITY 2.5 You have been asked to contribute to a discussion your class is to have on the subject of vivisection. You need to prepare what you are going to say in standard English. You will need to:

● give your audience some *information* about vivisection
● *describe* some aspects of the practice of vivisection
● *explain* what you think about the practice.

Hints

♦ Read the question carefully. Identify the words which refer to purpose, form and audience.
♦ You will also need to focus on:
   – tone
   – diction
   – syntax
   – structural features
   – linguistic features.
♦ Keep in mind the main focus of this activity – to write in a certain, chosen style.

Unit 2.6

Forms of writing

The unit activity is to write an article (see page 77).

Extract

A

It was reported by DSP that there had been a number of complaints from customers coming to the front desk about the standard of dress, and particularly the wearing of piercing jewellery.

JRR felt that things had reached an unacceptable low and that the way some staff were turned out was intimidating and inappropriate.

MCB said she thought the experiment had actually failed and that the rule for Fridays should be rescinded.

Extract

B

To: All staff
From: JL
Date: 23 December 20—
Subject: Staff dress code

Will staff please note that, as from 2 January, 'dressing down' on Fridays will not be permitted. All staff are expected to be appropriately and properly attired at all times. Male office staff are expected to wear ties.

Extract

C

At last business people the world over are finally coming to their senses … it's official; 'Dress Down Friday is Dead' and 'Dress Up Friday' has arrived if you want to keep your job. …
The Sunday Times in the UK reports that many of the global banking corporations are about to abolish 'dress down' in favour of more appropriate traditional formal attire. … Phew!

For all passionate and dedicated followers of textiles and fashion this can only spell good news and allows us to get on with what we are good at … the pursuit of excellence in cloth quality, construction and design.

Holland & Sherry News
September 2001
The Merino Trail
Autumn/Winter 2001 Collection

from www.hollandandsherry.com/news/2001/september

Making a start

You may be asked simply to write an essay, to explain or to describe something, but often the question in the exam, or for coursework, asks for a particular form of writing, for example:

- *Write an account of …*
- *Write an article explaining …*
- *Write a letter to a friend to describe ….*

You have written in a variety of forms already in this section: an account, a leaflet, a report and the text of a speech – all to inform, explain and describe.

The National Curriculum lists a wide range of forms which should be covered:

> 'to inform, explain and describe, focusing on conveying information and ideas clearly. The forms for such writing should be drawn from memos, minutes, accounts, information leaflets, prospectuses, plans, records, summaries.'

To fulfil most requirements the question will expect you to produce a substantial piece of writing. It is unlikely, therefore, that the ultimate task would be a memo or the minutes of a meeting, but they might form the basis of, or part of, a more substantial task. Look at the examples opposite of some forms of writing.

PURPOSE, FORM AND AUDIENCE

'Written texts are shaped by choices of **purpose**, **form** and **reader**. These elements are interdependent so that, for example, forms are adapted to the writer's aim and the intended reader.'

from The National Curriculum for English

Any piece of writing you are asked to do should contain all of these aspects, and you need to keep them all in mind when writing:

- The primary purposes, in this section, are to inform, explain and describe – either singly or in combination (Units 2.1–2.3).
- We have also examined the issue of the reader or audience (Unit 2.4).
- The focus of this unit is on different forms of writing.

Activity 2.6a

1 Name the form of writing you think each extract opposite represents.
2 Write a few sentences about each extract to explain how they are distinctive. You will be looking at linguistic and structural features.

Think about the form in which you are writing for each task you do. Here are some examples of linking a task to a form:

1 An **account** of my time at primary school
2 A **leaflet** which gives information on how to stop smoking
3 A **summary** of what my Saturday job entails
4 A piece of writing which describes our **plan** for a camping weekend
5 A **leaflet** about a local beauty spot for tourists
6 A **speech** which describes inner city poverty
7 A half-time **summary** of a football match for local radio
8 An **account** of the interesting parts of my work experience week
9 A **pamphlet** promoting recycling or vegetarianism
10 A **record** of a sailing trip or tour of North Wales
11 A **letter** asking a friend to stay
12 An **article** for my local newspaper explaining why we need more facilities for young people.

Activity 2.6b

1 Suggest a purpose for the writing in examples 1, 3, 5, 7, 8, 9, 10, 11, just as there is for 2, 4, 6, and 12. You might use more than one word from the triplet.
2 Make up titles of your own for the following forms of writing which would fit writing to inform, explain, describe:

   a) prospectus   c) letter   e) account
   b) article   d) report

SOME FORMS OF WRITING

memo Short for *memorandum*. An informal record, communication or reminder, informal diplomatic or business communication.

minutes The official record of the proceedings of a meeting.

account An explanation of reasons, causes, grounds or motives; report of facts or events.

article A non-fiction literary piece of writing forming an independent part of a publication, such as a magazine or newspaper.

leaflet Usually a single sheet of paper containing written matter, for example, advertising, information.

report Writing which describes an event or experience.

prospectus A written statement giving details of an organisation or enterprise usually with clients or customers in mind

plan A written account of a design, project, intention or aim.

record Authentic, written evidence of an event; the relating or commemoration of something recalled.

summary A concise but comprehensive account of the main points of something.

pamphlet Writing, in prose, on a subject of current interest or debate.

Read Unit Activity 2.6 on page 77 carefully.

Planning your writing
Gathering ideas

Activity 2.6c   Brainstorm some ideas for Unit Activity 2.6.

Hints   Here are some ideas to help you with the brainstorm:

- Look again at Extracts A and B (you could improvise a role play of the meeting to augment the material for the assignment).
- 'Dress Down Friday is a fund raiser whereby employees are allowed to dress casually on Fridays for a fee. The money raised is to go to charities to help stem illiteracy in inner-city youth.' (from www.russellreadingroom.com/drs_dwn)
- Do some research on the Internet.
- Talk to people who work in offices.
- Contact local companies to ask for their policy and views on the subject.
- Read Extract D.

Extract D

Office dress: Up and down the codes

Even the most strait-laced UK firms have begun relaxing their dress codes and allowing staff into work without a suit.

But just as battalions of British workers are discovering the joys of 'business casual', it appears their American counterparts are starting to dress up again.

Mr W. Gates models the casual look

So do UK workers prefer to dress up, or dress down? Phillipa Bergin, 28, is a researcher for a City law firm. She prefers wearing a suit.

What do you wear? I wear suits most of the time. I've got four and just rotate them. It's very easy. I dress down occasionally – say on a Friday if I'm going away for the weekend straight from work.

How do you feel? I know dressing down is supposed to make you feel more relaxed and release your creativity and so on, but I've dressed down occasionally and didn't find it made any difference at all. A friend says 'loose dress, loose attitude'. But I don't find that either – well, not unless I've been to the pub.

Luke Nolan, 33, works in the foreign exchange department of a City bank. He would like to go totally casual.

What do you wear? It's not total casual here, it's business casual with very strict rules – no denim, no running shoes, and you must wear a shirt with a collar.

Ideally, I'd dress completely differently.

How do you feel? I couldn't say that dressing down has made any difference at all, no. It hasn't made any difference to the work we do. But at a previous office where I worked, you could wear whatever you liked. People did seem more relaxed there. But that's probably symptomatic of the relaxed atmosphere of a firm which lets you wear what you want.

adapted from BBC News Online, 7 April 2000, http://news.bbc.co.uk/1/hi/uk/705135.stm

Paragraph plan

Activity 2.6d   Plan your article for the unit activity, focusing in particular on the form of the writing.

Hints   Your plan might look like this:

- **Paragraph 1: Introduction**
  Show that you understand the question. Bring your readers in with a lively introduction. Indicate that you have understood purpose and audience.
- **Paragraph 2: Explain the thinking behind 'Dress Down Friday'**
  Use material from your research. Present evidence. Use examples, witnesses and their views.

- **Paragraph 3: Report on reasons for its abolition**
  Use the research material. Add your own considered thoughts. Broaden the response to general, ethical matters if possible.
- **Paragraph 4: Conclusion**
  Remember this is not an argument. Make a rounded, general conclusion. Perhaps reiterate an interesting point, for example, the 'charity' aspect of the idea.

WHAT EXAMINERS ARE LOOKING FOR

In the exam:

- at grade C: 'a formal article, the tone of which is appropriately balanced'
- at grade A: 'a formal letter, the tone of which is appropriately serious'

In coursework:

- at grade C: 'adapt forms to different audiences and purposes'
- at grade A: 'a variety of writing forms such as the journalistic article or revelatory letter'.

Serious practice

Now you have planned your article, complete the unit activity.

UNIT ACTIVITY 2.6   The following has appeared in the brochure of a leading cloth merchant:

> '*The Sunday Times* in the UK reports that many of the global banking corporations are about to abolish "dress down" in favour of more appropriate traditional formal attire.'

> Write an article for a fashion magazine which explains the thinking behind 'Dress Down Friday' and describe how people responded. Go on to report what might have been the reasons for its abolition

WHAT SORT OF WRITING IS THIS ASSIGNMENT GOING TO PRODUCE?

- The writing assignment for this unit is **explanatory**, as designated in the unit activity.
- It is also going to be **descriptive** in part, probably concerning what people wear when they 'dress down' or otherwise.
- **Information**, perhaps to a lesser extent, will also be given – the picture of Bill Gates is informative.

- You will also be **reflecting** on what you and others think of the issue.
- It is also a **discursive** piece because it proceeds by reasoning, research and evidence rather than being made-up, imagined or intuited.
- It is also an **article**. The dictionary defines an article as *literary composition (other than fiction)*. So there is scope for well-crafted expression and an extended vocabulary.

Hints   Read the question carefully. Identify the words which refer to purpose, audience and form:

- you are to write an article
- you are also asked to report
- you will probably include some summary
- keep in mind your readership
- keep in mind the purposes of your writing.

Look back at previous units for help and guidance.

Unit 2.7

Planning your writing

The unit activity is to write an essay (see page 81).

Extract **A**

Many women do not know about the health dangers of smoking, according to a survey published on Thursday.

The Smoking Cessation Action in Primary Care (Scape) surveyed 1,757 men and women who were smokers or ex-smokers.

Figures show that 14-year-old girls are twice as likely to smoke as their male peers. It also showed that last year, lung cancer overtook breast cancer as the biggest killer of women.

But the Scape study showed 8 per cent of women did not believe smoking was linked to increased risk of lung cancer.

A quarter of those surveyed did not know smoking increases the risk of heart disease and two-thirds do not believe the habit increases the risk of miscarriage.

Ageing

To show women what might happen to them, two twins, aged 22, were made up to show how they would look at 40 if one smoked and the other did not.

The smoker had stained teeth and more wrinkles.

Just under a third of women told the survey they did not want to stop smoking because they were worried about putting on weight.

adapted from BBC News Online, 27 September 2001,
http://news.bbc.co.uk/1/hi/health/1566191.stm

Making a start

Writing to inform, explain and describe is assessed, depending on the exam board, for both coursework and examination.

*   If the writing task is for coursework then you have time to plan, draft and revise fully and properly. The procedure you adopt will depend on whether you are using a computer or writing by hand.
*   In an examination, the situation is different, but that does not mean that you do not plan your work.

Planning, redrafting and checking are the most important aspects of writing and the most neglected.

Activity 2.7a	1	Write a few sentences which describe your approach to planning, drafting and checking your work: a) for coursework b) in an exam. Write down what you usually do – or don't do.
	2	Compare this with others in the class. Decide where you need to improve.

There are a number of elements to planning and they need to be approached in a particular way.

Activity 2.7b

1 You are preparing for a writing assignment. Below are a number of activities which you will need to do. Sequence them in a useful order:

accuracy check	keyword list
additional research	notes on the topic
brainstorm	paragraph plan/table
copy-up and submit	proof-read
final draft	redraft
first draft	

Note: There may be more than one workable sequence.

2 The focus of these units is personal, original writing, not writing in response to a reading task or book you have read. How would the sequence change if you were writing an essay on *Romeo and Juliet*?

3 The National Curriculum states that students should 'plan, redraft and proof-read their work'. Do you think these processes are always needed for all writing you do? Explain your answer.

Activity 2.7c Read Extract A, which is a newspaper article.

1 Write a paragraph in your own words which shows that the article is written to inform, explain and describe.

2 Construct the brainstorm – a mind map, spider diagram or whichever method you are used to – from which this article could have been derived.

It is started for you here. A full spider diagram for this article would have lots of interconnected boxes.

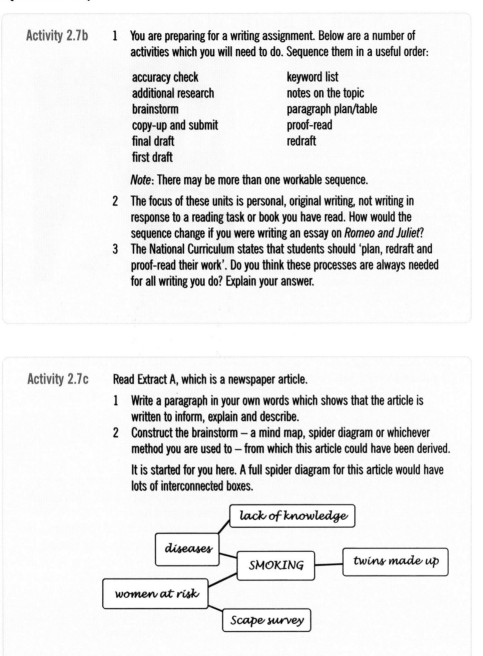

The power of words

At the planning stage, you should think about the words and phrases you are going to use. You will want to employ a vivid and extended vocabulary. This is particularly important when writing to describe.

Two sorts of discursive writing which lend themselves particularly to description are:

• travel writing
• biography.

Read Extract B which is an example of travel writing.

PLANNING AND DRAFTING
The National Curriculum has a number of things to say about planning and drafting:

'To improve and sustain their writing, pupils should be taught to:

a) plan, draft, redraft and proof-read their work on paper and on screen

b) judge the extent to which any or all of these processes are needed in specific pieces of writing

c) analyse critically their own and others' writing.'

from The National Curriculum for English

Planning and revising can be done simultaneously when working on a computer.

STARTING TO PLAN
Different names are given to the early stage of a writing assignment:

◆ gathering notes
◆ research
◆ brainstorming by mind-mapping, spider diagrams
◆ making word lists.

When planning, think about:

◆ the structure of your writing
◆ developing your vocabulary
◆ using rhetorical devices.

EXTENDING YOUR VOCABULARY
One way of extending your vocabulary is to use a thesaurus. However, you need to be sure that the alternative word *fits the context* of what you want to say and *fits your style* – otherwise it just looks as if you've used a thesaurus!

IMAGINATION

The Assessment Objectives for writing include the phrase: *communicate clearly and imaginatively*. This objective relates to all types of writing.

The word *imagination* does not mean *make it up* in this context. It means *to write in a way which constructs images in the mind of the reader*.

Extract B is true and real, but Gerald Durrell has made it vivid by the use of descriptive language. It is easier to do this when you are looking at something awesome. You are probably going to have to remember what things were like – use your imagination – in order to achieve a similar effect when you describe a place or person.

Extract B

A sea of headwaiters

Their numbers were prodigious, stretching to the furthermost horizon where they twinkled black and white in the heat haze.

We stood and watched the penguins, and they stood and watched us with immense respect and interest. As long as we stayed near the vehicle they showed no fear. The greater proportion of birds were, of course, adult; but each nesting burrow contained one or two youngsters, still wearing their baby coats of down, who regarded us with big, melting dark eyes, looking rather like plump and shy debutantes clad in outsize silver-fox furs. The adults, sleek and neat in their black and white suits, had red wattles round the base of their beaks and bright predatory, street-peddler eyes. As you approached them, they would back towards their burrows, twisting their heads from side to side in a warning display, until sometimes they would be looking at you completely upside down.

from The Whispering Land *by Gerald Durrell*

Activity 2.7d
The subject of Extract B is penguins. The text is informative and descriptive.

1 Make a list of vivid descriptive words and phrases, images and extended vocabulary used by Gerald Durrell in Extract B.

2 Look back at the brainstorm analysis you did for Extract A in Activity 2.7c. Add some descriptive or emotive words to the mind map, for example:

vulnerable
danger
hazard
peril
lives in jeopardy

women at risk

You can see that, even before you make a first, readable draft, you can have lots of ideas and words planned and prepared.

Read Unit Activity 2.7 on page 81 carefully.

Planning your writing

Gathering ideas

Activity 2.7e   Brainstorm the topic of Unit Activity 2.7.

◆ For your brainstorm (Activity 2.7e), you could use a list constructed as a table, with two columns headed *Good aspects of school* and *Bad aspects of school*, or a spider diagram.

◆ Make notes on the basic ideas in the brainstorm – people, places, events and experiences associated with the basic ideas.

◆ You might want additional research by asking others what their experiences are, or were, about school.

Paragraph plan

Activity 2.7f
1. Write a paragraph plan to give your ideas structure.
2. Having planned the assignment, now write a first draft.
3. Look back to Activity 2.7b.
   a) What stage are you at?
   b) What do you need to do next?

Hints

♦ Decide on the best places to put anecdotes, descriptions of people, interviews, etc.
♦ Remind yourself of Activity 2.7d: enhance your proposed sections with interesting words and phrases, for example, people you met or meet at school should be vividly described, as should some of your thoughts and feelings about them. There are lots of marks for an extended vocabulary. Make lists. Use a thesaurus, but with care.

WHAT EXAMINERS ARE LOOKING FOR

In the exam:

♦ at grade C: 'evidence of structure with usually coherent paragraphs'
♦ at grade A: 'coherently structured with fluently linked paragraphs ... evidence of conscious crafting'

In coursework:

♦ at grade C: 'reflective writing is well organised'
♦ at grade A: 'ideas are well organised, well formed and compelling'.

If you have done this thoroughly, you have a good foundation for a successful assignment.

Serious practice

Now you have planned your essay, complete the unit activity.

UNIT ACTIVITY 2.7 You are going to write a coursework assignment. It is to be a semi-autobiographical essay which may be published in your school magazine.

The title is: 'School! The best of it and the worst.'

Hints

♦ Read the question carefully. Identify the words which refer to the purpose, form and audience.
♦ What do you think *semi-autobiographical* means?

ASSESSMENT CRITERIA

The syllabus which you are following in English contains assessment criteria against which your teacher or the examiner will mark your work. Here are two which are relevant to Unit Activity 2.7:

♦ For a mark in Grade C: 'biographical and autobiographical accounts are presented with some originality, perhaps drawing on the experience of other writers. Such accounts employ descriptive and explicative techniques to good effect.'
♦ For a mark in Grade A: 'biographical and autobiographical pieces show an originality of approach and sophisticated treatment of subject-matter'.

Unit 2.8

Effective openings

The unit activity is to write openings for three different questions (see page 85).

Extract **A**

If you wouldn't do this to a dog,
WHY DO IT TO A FISH?

No one would consider doing to a dog what some so casually do to fish — trick them into impaling themselves in the mouth and pulling them into an environment where they can't breathe. But the fact is — fish feel pain just as all animals do.

from www.peta.org

Extract **B**

What other area of the country has more to offer than the Lake District National Park? It is the biggest of England's National Parks. Its 2,292 square kilometre area is best loved for the variety and contrast of its landscape. Here you can see high fells, rocky crags, lush green dales with long still lakes, vibrant villages and quiet hamlets.

from www.lake-district.gov.uk

Extract **C**

Many people have different hobbies. My hobby is astronomy, the science of the heavenly bodies. I find the enigma of the stars and their heavenly movements a conundrum, a riddle which I have been able to unravel ....

Extract **E**

On 24th September orders were given for the attack to be made the next day, 25th September. Jack knew of this. He knew that he might be killed. He was in command of 'C' Company and had to lead the attack. In the morning of 24th September about 10.30 a.m. he wrote his last letter. They were to move forward up to the line in the dark and occupy switch trenches ready for the attack. They were to be the second wave. The first wave were expected to have attained their objective and gone forward. He wrote in pencil a letter home and put it in his valise. It moves me to tears even now when I read it.

from The Family Story *by Lord Denning*

Extract **D**

Drugs, sex and rock and roll. That's the way the youth of the sixties and seventies are portrayed; that was their mantra. But is it any different today? Our survey for *Birmingham Today* suggests that things haven't changed that much ...

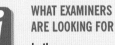 **WHAT EXAMINERS ARE LOOKING FOR**

In the exam:

- at grade C: 'an understanding of the topic'
- at grade A: 'a complete grasp of the topic'; 'engage the reader with clarity and detail'

In coursework:

- at grade C: 'writing which describes or explains is likely to engage reader response'
- at grade A: 'demonstrate a variety of styles which engages the reader'.

Making a start

The opening paragraph, in fact the opening sentence, is where you will make the first impression on your reader. A good opening will:

- entice your reader to read on
- engage your reader with your text and your purpose
- impress the marker of your coursework or the examiner of your paper.

Writing to inform, explain and describe, which would usually be designated as non-fiction writing, requires a number of things in the opening:

- a title
- an opening paragraph which:
    - provides evidence that you understand the topic or question
    - engages the reader's attention
    - is a launch-pad for the development of your ideas.

These are mainly concerned with content, but your opening should also:

- establish the tone of your writing
- show some aspects of your writing style
- indicate that you have a developed vocabulary.

Activity 2.8a

1 Match the strategies below with the requirements noted above:

   a) Look carefully at the actual task/question set.
   b) Decide whether your topic will be light-hearted, serious, reflective….
   c) End your paragraph with an open question or marker such as *and that was a day I shall never forget.*
   d) Think about using a three-word sentence.
   e) Employ technical terms or vivid description.
   f) Start with an uncompromising, attacking statement.

2 Look back at the openings of extracts in previous units:

   a) 'Seat belts' (Unit 2.1)
   b) 'Looking after your horse' (Unit 2.2)
   c) 'The whispering land' (Unit 2.3)
   d) Extract E in Unit 2.5.

   Write a few sentences explaining how each writer has employed the strategies noted above.

3 In pairs or groups, review the openings you wrote for Unit Activity 2.4.

   a) How successful were your openings and why?
   b) Which of the above strategies did you use?

KEY PHRASES
Make sure you understand these key phrases used by exam boards in relation to openings:

engage the reader
Here are some words which mean the same as engage in this context: *absorb, engross, grip, involve, captivate, draw in, fascinate.*

clear identification with purpose and audience
Identification here means to make the opening fit, to make a connection between the topic, the purpose and the reader.

begins to sustain reader response
Following on from the idea of engaging the reader, this suggests that good writing will elicit a response from the reader – usually a thinking response, but maybe some action too.

show an understanding of the topic
It is essential, especially in an examination, that you understand the point of the topic and show this in your opening. You need to show that you comprehend what the issue is about.

use an increasingly ambitious vocabulary
The more interesting your words, the more *enterprising, challenging* and *bold* they are, the more marks you will be awarded.

Titles

The title is part of your opening. You might write your title last, when you know exactly the contents of your writing.

A title should be:

- brief
- appropriate
- eye-catching
- informative.

The title might sum up the article, account or essay. Or it might be humorous, if that is appropriate.

Puns

One form of humour is to use a **pun** in a title. Here are some puns:

- *On track to be late again*
- *Curry favour at supper time*
- *A slick way to clean the beaches*
- *A hobby fit for the stars*
- *Is your swing driving you mad?*
- *Belt up and be safe!*
- *A Life in the Day of John Smith*
- *He was a legend in his own lunchtime.*

Activity 2.8b

1   Work in pairs or groups.
    Read Extracts A–E. Discuss how far each extract fulfils the considerations for openings listed in the table. Make a copy of the table to record your answers.
    Make notes of your discussion so you can report back to the class.

The opening:	Extract				
	A	**B**	**C**	**D**	**E**
provides evidence that the topic or question is understood					
engages the reader's attention					
is a launch pad for the development of ideas					
establishes a tone					
shows some initial aspects of writing style					
indicates a developed vocabulary					

2   Look at the guidance about titles given in this unit.

   a) Make up titles for Extracts B–E.
   b) Suggest the topics which would fit the puns given.

Serious practice

UNIT ACTIVITY 2.8 Write *openings* for each of the questions below.

1 Coursework assignment:
   Write an account of your work experience week, or of your part-time job, to be included in the Year 10 magazine. You should provide information about where you went and describe some of the people you met.

2 Examination question:
   It has been suggested that television 'soaps' are either obsessed with unrealistic glamour or too depressing to be healthy. Write an essay which explains your views on the subject.

3 Coursework or examination title: 'My perfect day'
   This is a free-choice question. For example, you could write about:

   - Watching a football match
   - A visit to my uncle
   - Retail therapy.

Hint

Read each question carefully. Identify the words which refer to purpose, form and audience in each case.

SOME EXAMPLES
Consider this advice before you tackle the unit activity.

◆ Use a spider diagram in the same way you would for a full assignment. Write appropriate ideas, words and phrases in each of the designated spaces.

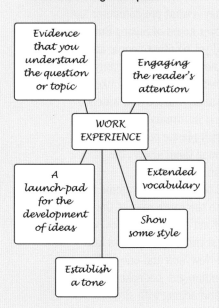

◆ The account of work experience is often set – and is often done poorly. Make a real attempt to fulfil these considerations, especially engaging the reader's attention, establishing a tone and employing an interesting vocabulary. Your opening should leave your reader wanting to read the rest of the account.

◆ Here is an example of an opening which informs, explains and describes a part-time job:

Miserable. Cold and damp it was; and no escape. If I wanted the computer games, season ticket and new trainers, there was only one bitter, biting, bleak, February way to get them. Work. A sack full of work. Not a Father Christmas sack to delight the eyes of little children. But a sack of news; gloom, doom and despair from around the world. But it's money – and not bad money at that. It wasn't boring work; there was usually something interesting, even exciting, happening, even at 6.30 in the morning ... like a couple of weeks ago.

WORK ON-SCREEN
You may be writing on-screen, using a computer.

It is best to collect notes, research and brainstorm material on paper before using a computer. This is true for all aspects of your writing task, including the opening.

There are a number of advantages of word-processing your writing:

◆ It is easy to edit and redraft because you don't need to rewrite everything.
◆ You can use a range of structural devices to maximum effect:
   – different fonts
   – indentation
   – tables
   – Word art and effects, and you could insert illustrations to enhance your work.

But there are also dangers with writing on-screen:

◆ Spell checks do not solve spelling problems.
◆ Grammar checks do not solve grammar problems.
◆ Ultimately you are being marked for your own, original, standard English, continuous prose writing and not for the sophistication of your computer software.

There is a strong argument shared by many examiners that writing assignments and tasks are best done by hand.

Unit 2.9

Developing your writing

The unit activity is to write an essay (see page 89).

New Mexico, October 1968

Sunrise had just begun on Route 66 and the man and his wife sat as one in the dust beside the long, black road, his broad-brimmed hat over his eyes, her shawl cocooning them both against the cold. They did not move or speak. They waited. 5

Behind them, in an infinity of screaming colours, lay their America, an America known only to them and not to those who drove thunderingly by; a silent and beautiful land without cities or shopping malls or billboards, 10 just the Painted Earth and its mountains and mesas, rivers and lakes and canyons and great red rocks, like cathedrals; and trees, stillborn and black. And beyond that, the sun.

This is the desert: the America of the First 15 Americans, who call themselves simply *Dineh*. The Spanish conquistadores knew them as *Apaches de Navajo* and the settlers called them redskins; and they have been waiting beside this long road for a century or more, since Colonel 20 Kit Carson came with his United States Army, marching against them into the Canyon of Death, destroying, as he went, their mud homes and their livestock and starving them into surrender and into signing treaties: which granted them no 25 more than the worst of their own lands, renamed, with ignominy, reservations.

No other people have been more mythologized than they – what pre-computer age Western child had never heard of Sitting Bull 30 and Geronimo? – and yet no other people are more forgotten. And nowhere does this irony echo louder than among themselves. Dressed like cowboys, they have waited, wasted and watched their children play that interminable game based 35 on themselves, but with plastic bows and arrows and the strongest among them always the triumphant white man.

It was a national television programme that persuaded me to go to the south-west of the 40 United States, to Arizona and New Mexico, where the Navajo, the largest tribe, live. It was a late show broadcast from New York and one of the guests was a young Indian girl, bedecked in feathers, and beads and aching with shyness. 45

continued

The compere said: 'Well, folks, we have a *gen-u-ine* Indian princess for you tonight, just like Hiawatha. Let's hear it now for Miss American Indian of 1968!'

He put on an Indian head-dress and danced a bizarre dance in front of her and the audience laughed. 50

'Tell me, honey,' he said to her, 'why you come here to heap big paleface pow-wow?'

There was a long silence before she said, 'I have been sent to ask for jobs for my people and for food for our hungry children and for freedom and honour.' The compere was speechless; a commercial followed quickly. 55

The average income of an Indian family is less than half that of even a black family, and in remote areas, in the 1960s, it was not uncommon for five people to attempt to survive on the equivalent of £250 a year, or less. Then, an 60

Indian could expect to be dead at forty-three or twenty-seven years sooner than a white American, and an Indian child was twice as likely as a white child to die during infancy. Diseases under control in white America are rampant still on the reservations. Tuberculosis, which has all but extinguished a whole tribe in the State of Washington, is ten times the national average. 65 70

There is little work of any kind on the reservations. And because there is no work, one of the few ways they can make money is to sell hand-made jewellery and pottery to white tourists, the descendants of those who lured tribes off their land with trinkets and trade. Nowadays, many Indians are uneducated, untrained, illiterate; many live in less than slums, in dome-shaped structures of mud and wood, called hogans, and in tarpaper shacks and shelters made of leaves and tents. A high proportion of Indian families are divided because there is no transport into the outposts and the government boarding schools are far away and sometimes in another state. A statistic frequently used is that the suicide rate among Indian teenagers is one hundred times that of the rest of the country, and suicide occurs as early as eight years old. 75 80 85 90

I drove on to Navajo land at dawn when the desert is spectacular. The old man and woman huddled by the road were glad of my offer of a lift: they had been there all night, and they spoke no English, and in haphazard Spanish they said they wanted to go to a trading post to buy food. 95

from Heroes *by John Pilger*

Making a start

Having something to say

When you have established an effective opening, you will move on to the *substance* of your writing. For coursework and exam, this needs to be a

COURSEWORK OR EXAM?

Writing to inform, explain and describe may be set as a coursework assignment or exam question, depending on the examination board specification.

◆ A coursework assignment allows you the time and freedom to do lots of research, revising, editing and polishing of your text.

◆ In an examination you have no facility for research. However, your writing is still expected to be *developed* and *substantial*. You must allocate time in an exam for planning and for thinking in order to properly develop the substance of your writing.

Note:

◆ The number of marks available for writing is *equal* to those available for responding to the reading extracts.

◆ In an exam writing question, at least *one-third* of the time should be spent thinking and planning.

If your writing contains simple assertions supported by rather ordinary anecdotes or examples and never pushes the topic to a higher level of engagement for the reader, it will receive a low mark. If you extend the ideas to a general, moral level which forces the reader to really think, then the result will be more satisfying.

developed and substantial section. In this, the main body of your text, you will need to show that you can:

- develop your writing into a substantial text
- organise your text into a coherent shape which enhances its content
- provide detail from research material or other sources
- present generalised explanations, descriptions, impressions
- vary content to keep the reader engaged
- sustain interest through to your ending.

These factors are mainly concerned with the content of your writing – what you are communicating, the ideas, points of view, observations, thoughts, feelings, impressions, facts and opinions.

Activity 2.9a	Read the extract by John Pilger carefully. Working in pairs, answer the following questions. They will re-cap some of the things you have been doing.

1 In what ways does the writing inform, explain and describe?
2 Who do you think John Pilger's audience might be?
3 What is the tone and style of the writing?
4 What would you say was the form of the writing?
5 Why do you think Pilger's opening is good?
6 What do you notice about the ending?

Looking at the detail

We are concerned in this unit with the *content* of writing – the substance, the ideas, the actual material – what the writer is saying. You are now going to make a detailed analysis of the content of the John Pilger extract.

Activity 2.9b	Read the extract by John Pilger again so you are familiar with its content. Then answer the following questions. Make sure your answers are *detailed*.

1 **Paragraph 1, lines 1–5**
   a) What information do you get about time and place?
   b) What is the effect of the introduction of the two characters?

2 **Paragraph 2, lines 6–14**
   a) What is the subject of this paragraph?
   b) What point is being made by the phrase 'known only to them'?
   c) Who are the other people implied in this paragraph?
   d) What hint do you get of Pilger's viewpoint in this paragraph?

3 **Paragraph 3, lines 15–27**
   a) What is first specific subject-matter of this paragraph?
   b) What becomes the subject-matter?
   c) How does this paragraph link with the previous writing?
   d) What historical information, explanation and description can you find?
   e) Distinguish between fact and opinion in this paragraph.
   f) How does Pilger begin to make a general, moral point here?

4 **Paragraph 4, lines 28–38**
   a) How does Pilger develop his subject in this paragraph?

contd

Activity 2.9b contd

b) How does he link the past to his present audience?

c) How does Pilger use an ironic anecdote to make a general, moral point?

d) Explain how Pilger is providing information, description and explaining what the Indians do, but also forming and framing the reader's sympathies. What is the substance of these sympathies?

5 **Paragraph 5, lines 39–59**

a) How does the use of anecdote here develop the subject and theme of the writing?

b) How do the two characters contrast and engage the reader?

c) How has Pilger developed and manipulated the sympathies of the reader in this paragraph with the Indian girl?

d) In what ways has Pilger introduced a moral, ethical or social element into his writing by this stage. What is it?

6 **Paragraphs 6 and 7, lines 60–91**

Consider the content of these two paragraphs under the following headings:

- Development of subject and theme using facts and explanation
- Use of historical authority, social facts and detail
- Use of contrast and comparison to develop ideas, theme, issues
- Use of irony and emotion.

7 **Paragraph 8, lines 92–97**

In terms of content, why is the 'ending' paragraph satisfying?

CONTENT AND STYLE

Activity 2.9b is intended to focus your analysis on content.

However, it is impossible to consider a piece of writing, much less to create a piece of writing, without a consideration of both content *and* style.

The words used by John Pilger – his diction – are inextricably tied up with his subject-matter. Both are critical elements in the effect of the writing.

Look at the first sentence again and think about the significance of the word *cocooning*, both in its specific sense and as a metaphor for the plight of the Indian people.

Serious practice

UNIT ACTIVITY 2.9 Write an essay to be included in an Oxfam publication for people your age. The title is 'Nairobi 2003'.

Hints

- Read the question carefully. Identify the words which refer to the purpose, form and audience.
- Use the information you found for Unit Activity 2.4.
- The structure of the article should follow that used by John Pilger:

Paragraph 1: Opening
Set the time and place, make it immediate and personal.

Paragraph 2: Establishing the issue
Describe the living conditions and education facilities.

Paragraph 3: Develop the issue
Some informative historical background, interview or anecdote.

Paragraph 4: Develop and generalise the issue
Explanation and description in more detail, anecdote or examples of deprivation, compare with other places, for example, children in the UK and their facilities, moral responsibility of us all.

Paragraph 5: Sustain the issue – emotive input
Moving interview with mother and children, statistics of neglect, possibilities for the future, social neglect, fears and hopes.

Paragraph 6: Ending
Come back to the time and place.

WHAT EXAMINERS ARE LOOKING FOR

In the exam:

- at grade C: 'paragraphs are competently linked by content and language'
- at grade A: 'writing is well structured and developed, achieving clarity and coherence'

In coursework:

- at grade C: 'paragraphs make meanings clear and coherent'
- at grade A: 'paragraphs are well constructed and linked to clarify the organisation of the writing'.

Unit 2.10

Writing technique: language and layout

The unit activity is exam practice in writing to inform, explain and describe (see page 93).

This extract is from an article on the changing British countryside:

The Foot and Mouth outbreak of 2001 devastated the rural life of the country. Government statisticians say it was the worst ever. Bruised and battered, Britain's farmers saw their life's work and savings ebb away like a retreating spring tide. This once green and pleasant island became a no-man's-land where not only the farming community suffered but travel, leisure, country sports and tourism declined too.

Who will rejuvenate the farmsteads of England? Who will tend the hedgerows and be guardians of the common land? Somebody must do something.

We spoke to Tom Weston, third generation farmer, on a lush, buttercup strewn meadow which once provided prime, gourmet food for his herd of prize Frisians.

'It's not like an episode of "The Archers",' says Tom, 'where you can write a script and make it all come right.'

Tom's herd no longer graze the lush, green meadow – they lie putrefying in an underground trench miles away – culled in order to 'ring fence' the epidemic and because of government bureaucracy. Not one of his animals had the disease. Madness. And now the feed companies and the banks want their money and the future speaks of diversification.

Tom's wife cries and lies to the creditors: the supermarkets import *le boeuf de France*.

Making a start

It is obvious from reading the John Pilger extract in Unit 2.9 that the content and overall arrangement of material is an important part of a successful piece of writing; but it is also obvious that there are other crucial elements to writing. John Pilger's ability to use language is perhaps most striking.

Apart from detailed content, your writing will need to show skilful use of the following elements – all of which adds up to **style**:

- diction and imagery
- linguistic features/rhetorical devices ⎤ language
- structural features ⎤ layout
- presentational features.

Diction and imagery

Diction is the words you use. You should try always to employ an extended vocabulary, vivid verbs, adverbs and adjectives and use words and phrases which appeal to and engage the senses of the reader. Imagery (the use of simile, metaphor, personification, hyperbole) is also a compelling way to enrich your writing. Sometimes the deliberate use of cliché can be effective, too.

Linguistic features/rhetorical devices

These features include:

- the rhetorical question
- assertion
- lists
- command
- dialogue/direct speech
- inclusion
- rhyme and rhythm

- allusion
- emotive language
- irony, satire
- authoritative reference
- contradiction
- signpost words and phrases
- anecdote.

See page 92 for more about linguistic features.

Structural features

Structural features are the different ways writing can be put together, depending on the form, purpose and audience. For example:

- varied lengths of paragraph
- varied lengths of sentence
- false sentence (for example, one word)
- indentation

- bullet points
- bold font
- headings and subheadings
- varied position of topic sentence.

There is more about structural features on page 93.

Presentational features

Presentational features create the overall visual effect and design. The writing may be enhanced with photographs, cartoons, tables, graphs, and so on. A newspaper story, pamphlet or leaflet might require specific and well-designed presentational features.

WHAT EXAMINERS ARE LOOKING FOR

In the exam:

- at grade C: 'competent use of modifiers, discursive markers and a developing vocabulary'
- at grade A: 'evidence of a fluent control of a range of devices and discursive markers together with an extended vocabulary'

In coursework:

- at grade C: 'style and vocabulary used to create effect and sustain reader interest'
- at grade A: 'writing has assured control of style; vocabulary is ambitious'.

LINGUISTIC FEATURES

Rhetorical question
A question which does not genuinely seek an answer but which simply raises the issue, for example, *Why does the cold weather catch us ill-prepared every year?*

Assertion
This is another way of raising an issue and engaging an audience – by stating something boldly which might be contentious, for example, *Commuters should blame nobody but themselves for late trains ....*

Dialogue/direct speech
This can be used effectively in discursive writing as this unit shows. But it should be used sparingly and appropriately.

Inclusion
Using the pronouns *we* and *us* can be a way of including the reader in the issue, for example, *We all remember what it's like to feel lonely ....*

Rhyme and rhythm
These can appear in prose writing as well as poetry. Well-balanced sentences and the distribution of syllables can produce rhythmic prose. Rhymes within sentences can be effective, for example, *The government are making and breaking their own rules.*

Allusion
Alluding to or making reference to something outside of the topic is effective, for example, *No mere snow drift would have stopped Auden's Night Mail crossing the border ....*

Activity 2.10a

1 Study the diagram below which takes two paragraphs from John Pilger's text and analyses some of the writing devices he used. You may be able to add something to the analysis.
2 Look at the lists of linguistic and structural features above and find some examples of these in the rest of Pilger's extract.
3 Choose two or three paragraphs from your essay for Unit Activity 2.9. Make an analysis of the writing in the same way as the example below. You may do this in pairs and on acetate so that it can be shared with the class.

Suggested personification   *List, vivid adjectives, alliteration*

Sunrise had just begun on Route 66 and the man and his wife sat as one in the dust beside the long, black road, his broad-brimmed hat over his eyes, her shawl cocooning them both against the cold. They did not move or speak. They waited.

Image related to major theme of plight of Indians – they are cocooned in a reservation

Effective, arresting short sentences

Assertion, passive voice, inclusion   *Rhetorical question*

No other people have been more mythologized than they – what pre-computer age Western child had never heard of Sitting Bull and Geronimo? – and yet no other people are more forgotten. And nowhere does this irony echo louder than among themselves. Dressed like cowboys, they have waited, wasted and watched their children play that interminable game based on themselves, but with plastic bows and arrows and the strongest among them always the triumphant white man.

Conjunction begins sentence

Rhythmic alliteration

Assertion

Irony linked to the theme of the writing   *Interesting adjective*

Activity 2.10b Find examples of the following linguistic and structural features in the extract on page 90:

- the rhetorical question
- assertion
- lists
- command
- dialogue/direct speech
- inclusion of the reader
- rhyme

- allusion
- varied lengths of paragraph
- varied length of sentence
- false sentences, short sentences, balanced sentences

- emotive language
- irony
- authoritative reference
- contradiction
- anecdote/related or shared experience.

The focus of this unit is on understanding and being able to apply appropriate features and devices to the raw material of your writing so that it is engaging and compelling.

- If you are writing a coursework assignment, your first draft should incorporate some of these aspects of writing.
- In an examination you will need to remember these features as you plan your answer.

> **Activity 2.10c** Using the information above and any more you already have or can find on the topic, design and write a leaflet intended for distribution on a forthcoming Countryside March.
>
> Use the structural and presentational features noted in this unit.

Serious practice

> **UNIT ACTIVITY 2.10** Exam practice: set a maximum time of 50 minutes from start to finish for this activity.
>
> *Either*:
>
> 1 Describe your favourite hobby or pastime to the readers of *Hobby Magazine*, explaining what you find stimulating about it.
>
> *Or*:
>
> 2 Write a letter to the newspaper which produced this headline describing the chaos in your area and explaining what you think should be done to prevent it.
>
> ### Snow Chaos
>
> We get caught out every time. One night's snowfall and the country gridlocks to a standstill.

SIGNPOSTS

You have met this term already in Units 1.3 and 1.9. The terms *connective*, *conjunction* and *discourse* marker are also used to mean the same thing.

A signpost is a word or phrase which links ideas in an appropriate way, for example:

furthermore
another aspect of ...

however
apart from that
another factor which ...
it has been assumed that
nevertheless
one way forward
in view of this fact.

Signposts should be an aspect of your writing but, like all things, should be used carefully and sparingly

STRUCTURAL FEATURES

Varied lengths of paragraph

This is good practice for establishing emphasis and an engaging overall structure. Paragraphing should have a purpose, and should enhance and clarify meaning.

Varied length of sentence and the false sentence

Short sentences can reinforce a desired tone and serve to agitate the reader. They may also arrest fluency for a desired reason. The one-word sentence is ungrammatical and should be used very sparingly.

Indentation and bullet points

When producing a leaflet or pamphlet, these devices may be useful and enhance presentation. Remember, however, that marks are awarded for your ability to write continuous prose in standard English.

Hints

- Read the question carefully. Identify the words which refer to the purpose, form and audience.
- Question 1: You might begin with an assertion: *Stamp collecting is the only thing for an intelligent human being to spend his time doing.*
- Question 2: You might begin with a flurry of devices: *Mayhem. Young, old, rich, poor, male and female – all helpless. Will we never learn?*

Unit 2.11

Effective endings

The unit activity is to practise writing some effective endings (see page 97).

Extract
A

This is the ending of an account of a Year 10 work-experience week which focused on a description of the different people encountered:

And so there we were. Friday afternoon and the last hour of the week. The gossip, bitchiness and back-biting was over; the friendliness and well meaning attention Michael had shown me had cost him dear. He had explained that he and Marcia would repair their differences and that life would go on. I felt a sense of guilt. I had learned nothing about banking but oceans about people and their pettiness and jealousies. I shall need to find out the denouement of the little soap opera I created.

Extract
B

This is the ending of a long account/investigation into the Hatfield train crash at Howe Dell. The final section is about blame and gives the example of a train disaster in 1915 when the culprits were imprisoned but pardoned. They both suffered nervous breakdowns. The writer concludes his investigation about Hatfield like this:

The politicians and their advisers who, in Corbett's phrase, 'ripped apart' Britain's railways have never spoken publicly about the crash at Howe Dell, though sometimes their successors in the Conservative Party have admitted that 'they got some things wrong'. They have directorships, they sit on boards, they have lunch at the club. So far as we know, they sleep soundly at night. A nervous breakdown or two would be just.

from Ian Jack, 'The 12.10 to Leeds' in Granta 73, Spring 2001

Extract
C

This is an article about an English theatre company which set up in a French village in 1991 in an area of declining population and employment:

M. Perrier, the local boy, now brings his troupe back to rehearse in Herisson, and sometimes to perform there. In the château above the village, there is an annual music festival. And M. Emmendoerffer hopes to attract other projects.

'Farming won't keep this village going in the future,' he says. 'But maybe theatre will.'

from The Times Magazine, 25 January 2003

Making a start

The concluding paragraph is often a neglected aspect of writing. Too often students either end their writing by trailing off or they simply stop. The object of this unit is to raise the profile of the ending.

Here are a number of synonyms for the word *ending* which show that there may be more to it than you might think:

- *cessation*
- *closure*
- *completion*
- *conclusion*
- *consummation*
- *culmination*
- *denouement*
- *resolution.*

Activity 2.11a	Working in pairs, discuss the words listed above. Then, using a good dictionary, write down a precise meaning for each word.

Hint For example, *consummation*, which is not often used in this context, means *to bring to completion in a perfect and satisfying way*. It may not always be your intention to do this. The people who write soap operas for television, writers such as Dickens and Hardy, writers of biography and travel writing often deliberately do not want an ending which is *perfect* and *satisfyingly complete*; they prefer to leave things on a knife-edge.

Make some similar comments about the other words.

Tone and style

The last paragraph of your writing is as important as the first. It is the last thing a reader experiences from your writing and it will either linger in his or her mind or be instantly forgettable.

You will already have established a tone and style in your writing. Consider these ideas:

- It would be coherent to end with a similar and consistent tone and style.
- It would be interesting to change or reverse the tone and style to make an effective ending.

Activity 2.11b	Look back to Unit 2.1 and re-read the article 'Seat belts'. In Unit 2.5 you were asked to decide on some words which described the style and tone of this article. You probably chose: *informative, factual, objective, detached, economical.*

1 Write a concluding paragraph for 'Seat belts' which continues in this tone and style.
2 Now write one which is descriptive, vivid, shocking, emotional and sentimental.
3 Note the difference and decide which is the best ending.

WHAT DOES THE ENDING OF A PIECE OF WRITING DO?

It may:

◆ provide a quick review
◆ restate information or an explanation
◆ reiterate key questions or issues
◆ summarise
◆ enforce
◆ provide a link elsewhere
◆ relate back
◆ join up to the topic sentence of the opening.

Planning your ending

The ending of your writing should be no less planned than the rest of it. There are a number of things to consider as you plan your ending; you have a number of choices. Your ending might:

- lift the writing, re-engaging the reader
- end on a question or exclamation
- leave the reader wanting more
- leave the reader agitated
- leave the reader satisfied
- achieve closure
- achieve roundness
- end on a knife-edge
- end outrageously.

Activity 2.11c Read carefully the examples of endings on page 94 (Extracts A–C) and the ending to the extract by John Pilger in Unit 2.9. Discuss each ending in turn and write notes about:

- the kind of ending each is
- the effect each ending would have on the reader
- the tone and style of the endings
- whether or not you think each ending is successful and why.

Activity 2.11d The form of your writing might be a relevant factor in the ending you choose to write.

Copy the table below. It will remind you of some of the things to keep in mind when writing endings for your assignments and some of the forms you might use.

Tick the boxes if you think the ending would particularly suit the form.

Your ending might:	Form							
	Article	Speech	Account	Letter	Leaflet	Report	Discursive essay	Other
lift the writing, re-engaging the reader								
end on a question or exclamation								
leave the reader wanting more								
leave the reader agitated								
leave the reader satisfied								
achieve closure								
achieve roundness								
end outrageously								
end on a knife edge								

Serious practice

You are going to practise writing endings. You have seen that there are different ways to end a piece of writing. Sometimes several aspects will happen at once. You can lift the ending by concluding with a question, or close the writing in a satisfying way, leaving the matter concluded.

You also need to decide on the tone and style of your ending, whether to make it consistent with the rest of the writing or effectively contrasting.

UNIT ACTIVITY 2.11

1   Choose **two** of the unit activities in Units 2.1–2.10 and re-read what you wrote. Pay particular attention to the ending.

   a) Think about the effectiveness of the ending and rewrite it to make it better.
   b) Change the ending deliberately to achieve one of the effects noted in this unit.
   c) Try altering the tone and style of the ending for effect.

2   Repeat the exercise for two more endings you have already written.

WHAT EXAMINERS ARE LOOKING FOR

In the exam:

- at grade C: 'conclude writing in a rounded and interesting way'
- at grade A: 'offer a stylish ending which is interesting and engaging'

In coursework:

- at grade C: 'show evidence of a planned and deliberate conclusion to writing'
- at grade A: 'attempt a sophisticated, original and satisfying ending'

Hints

Five tasks which might be very suitable for this activity are:

- Describing an unusual or memorable place (Unit 2.3)
- Children like us (Unit 2.4)
- Vivisection (Unit 2.5)
- Dress Down Friday (Unit 2.6)
- School, the best of it and the worst (Unit 2.7).

LINGUISTIC FEATURES

The ending of your writing should not neglect the linguistic features and devices you may have used elsewhere, such as:

- rhetorical questions
- ironic statements
- humour
- direct speech
- reference to authorities.

EFFECTIVE LANGUAGE

Remember that the final paragraph is as worthy as any other of containing:

- interesting and vivid vocabulary
- varied sentence lengths and constructions
- signpost words
- linguistic features and devices.

So remember what you have learned about **diction** and **syntax** (see Unit 2.5).

TOPIC SENTENCE

This may be at the beginning, middle or end of a paragraph.

When writing an ending, it might be effective to finish with the topic sentence. This would have the effect of relating back to the beginning, achieving a rounded conclusion.

Unit 2.12

*Bringing it
all together*

*The unit activity is to
practise the range of
skills and techniques
learned in Units 2.1–2.11
(see page 101).*

On women

The women of Venice are very handsome, and very vain. They are tall, they walk beautifully, and they are often fair. Their eyes are sometimes a heavy-lidded greenish-blue, like the eyes of rather despondent armadillos. Rare indeed is a dishevelled Venetian woman, and even the Madonna's and female saints of the old masters are usually elegantly dressed. The most slovenly people to be seen in the city are nearly always tourists.

The Venetians are not, by and large, rich: but they have always spent a large proportion of their money on clothes and ornaments, and you will hardly ever see a girl dressed for pottering, in a sloppy sweater and a patched skirt, or in that unpressed *déshabillé* that marks the utter emancipation of the Englishwoman. The girls at the university look more like models than academics: and the housemaids, when they walk off in scented couples for their weekend pleasures, would hardly seem out of place at Ascot or at a gala convention of the Women Lawyers Association.

Among the patrician ladies of old Venice, as among the women of Arabian harems, there was nothing much to think about but clothes and babies.

Clamped in their houses out of harm's way, they were little more than tools or playthings: even the Doge's wife had no official position. No item of dress was more popular among Venetian aristocrats than the absurd towering clogs, sometimes twenty inches high, which obliged their wives to totter about with the help of two servants.

This has left its legacy in the determination of modern Venetian women to wear the highest possible heels in all circumstances.

from Venice *by Jan Morris*

Making a start

Look at the summary of what you have studied and practised in Units 2.1–2.11. This has been done by focusing on each particular aspect through modelling successful writing. Then you have practised the skill yourself. Now it is time to pull these discrete aspects of writing together.

Activity 2.12a　Re-cap some of the things you have learned.

1   a) What is writing to inform mainly about?
    b) From which various sources does information come?
    c) What do you need to be able to do when writing to inform?

2   a) What will you be doing when you are writing to explain?
    b) List four different ways of explaining.

3   a) What should you aim to do when writing to describe?
    b) Where might you find writing which describes?

4   What are some of the things you should consider when thinking about the intended audience of your writing?

5   List six words which could describe the tone of a piece of descriptive writing.

6   a) How many forms of writing can you think of?
    b) Which forms of writing might you use when describing an expedition you went on to Australia which explained the difficulties experienced by the aborigines.

7   a) What does the National Curriculum say about planning and drafting?
    b) What different ways are there to plan your writing?
    c) How long should you spend in planning?

8   Why is it important to have a good opening?

9   What are the six things you need to show you are doing in the main, developed body of your writing?

10 What four writing techniques add up to your style?

11 List six things a good ending might do.

Activity 2.12b　Read the extract and then answer these questions:

1   Make a table or spider diagram which shows the information contained in the extract.

2   Put an asterisk against the information which is based upon impression or opinion.

3   What is explained in the final paragraph?

4   Find and note examples of description in the extract. Comment on the diction used.

5   What do you think is the likely audience for this text?

6   Is the extract age-specific, gender-specific, social-class-specific or specific in any other way?

7   Write several sentences using key words which describe the tone or mood of the writing

8   How would you describe the form of this piece of writing?

9   What would you need to change about, and add to, the text in order to change its form to a letter or a journal?

10 Draw a spider diagram which might have been the early brainstorm for this writing. The central box will contain the words *Venetian women*.

11 Comment on the title and the first sentence as an effective opening to the writing.

12 What different sources has Jan Morris used for the detailed development of the text?

13 Give examples of imagery and extended vocabulary used in the text.

14 Comment on the overall structure of the extract. How are paragraphs used?

15 Make a detailed analysis of stylistic features of the extract, as you did in Unit 2.10, page 92.

16 This piece of writing ends well. How?

KEY TERMS

Make sure you understand these terms.

voice

In the Jan Morris extract, the **voice** is that of the writer; they are her observations and impressions we are receiving. The tone of the piece reinforces this. She doesn't actually say that she is in Venice looking at the things she describes, but the **tone** strongly suggests this, as does the comment in the last paragraph.

person

The text is written in the **third person**. She refers to *them* and *they*. The writer does not appear in the text herself. She might have done so by writing, for example, *I have never seen a girl dressed for pottering ....* Instead she involves the reader by using the **second person**, *you*.

Serious practice

Write to inform, explain and describe in response to the following questions. You should choose either one coursework assignment or attempt both exam questions, depending on whether you are doing writing to inform, explain and describe for coursework or the exam.

WHAT EXAMINERS ARE LOOKING FOR

Whatever the level or grade of your writing, there will always be room for improvement. You should try to remember the following.

- The words chosen (the diction, vocabulary) should be varied and appropriate, extended and vivid.
- Sentences and paragraphs should show variety in their length and structure.
- Linguistic features and devices should be evident.
- Connectives should show varied ways of linking ideas, paragraphs and clauses.
- A range of punctuation should be evident, not just full stops and commas.
- Openings and endings should be engaging.
- Writing should be focused clearly at the intended audience and topic.
- Writing should show evidence of planning and a clear overall structure.
- There should be a high level of accuracy in punctuation and spelling.

UNIT ACTIVITY 2.12 Coursework assignments

1   You are the foreign correspondent for a news magazine. Choose a place which you have visited and liked, then research something of the history, people, sights and culture of the place.

Write an essay which informs, explains and describes your impressions in a way which will engage your readers' interest.

2   You have been asked to take part in a radio programme called 'The Moral Maze'. The topic is 'Transplantation and transgenics in the 21st century: have we gone too far?'

You will need to research your topic, but will probably already have some ideas about organ transplants between people and between humans and animals. Websites will provide lots more detail.

You need to:

- inform your audience of some facts
- explain some of the moral issues involved
- describe what you think might be the way forward.

Write out what you are going to say.

Examination questions

3   The issue of bad behaviour on the streets of your town has been raised recently in the local press.

- Inform the readers of your local newspaper about the lack of investment and facilities for young people in the area in which you live.
- Explain what you think is their responsibility.
- Describe what you would like to see happen.

4   Write the text of a leaflet which explains and describes the advantages of staying at a seaside town in the winter.

Review

What you have studied

Units 2.1–2.11 have been concerned with the following aspects of writing:

- understanding the purposes embodied in the terms inform, explain, describe
- being aware of your reader or audience
- understanding the relevance of tone and style
- exploring different forms of writing
- looking at planning, revising and editing your writing
- considering different openings and titles
- exploring the development and organisation of ideas
- using linguistic, structural and presentational features
- developing diction, vocabulary and imagery
- looking at effective endings.

What you have written

In Units 2.1–2.11, you may have written about any or all of the thirteen topics which have been suggested. It would be helpful to look some of them again in the light of what you have learned since.

In particular, bear in mind diction, vocabulary and imagery. Examiners reward students who use interesting, extended words, phrases and metaphors.

The diagram below summarises the components of writing you have been learning about and practising. Use it as a template for your own coursework assignments and examination practice. When you use it, make sure the boxes are big enough to jot down your ideas.

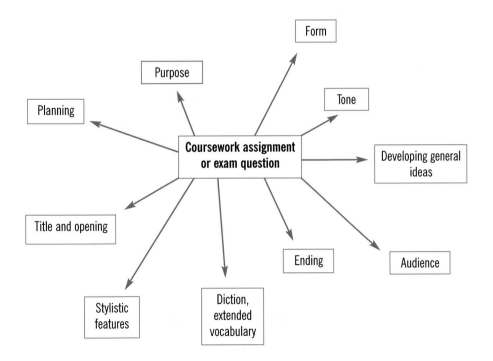

Unit 3.1

Writing to analyse

The unit activity is to write an analysis (see page 105)

Extract
A

There are undoubtedly some major advantages, to be gained by everybody, in the provision of a council skate park. To begin with, the park would not interfere with ordinary members of the public, so their disapproval, and their fear of the danger they feel themselves to be in from skateboarding in the street, would be removed. Furthermore, if the expertise of local clubs, semi-professionals and enthusiasts were sought, a state of the art terrain could be constructed which would bring kudos and even money – through competitions – to the town. It might also be felt desirable to build picnic areas, refreshment facilities and ancillary amusements to widen the appeal of the park to others. In this way, a considerable amenity would be set up around a central focal point – the skate park. Moreover, this would be a chance to utilise some currently under-used green areas outside the town centre. Congestion would be relieved and a sense of peace and tranquillity could be established.

On the other hand, there is a cost involved and it is essential that the cost is not passed on to the users of the park. This would be a killer blow. There would also be an unfortunate inclination to police the area. This should be avoided – the chance for self-regulation and supervision should be taken. Maintenance would need to be paid for, too, and insurance liability is another factor. Skateboarders are freedom-freaks. The idea of institutionalising their free spirit would be seen as a disadvantage – but the promise of some decent ramps might counterbalance this moral dilemma.

Making a start

Writing to analyse may involve you in a number of different approaches to a subject. Synonyms for the word *analyse* include:

- *estimate*
- *evaluate*
- *examine*
- *interpret*
- *investigate*
- *judge*
- *break down*
- *think through*.

Activity 3.1a	For each of the words listed above, write a question which indicates the need for analytical skills. For example:

1 *Estimate the cost of a weekend rambling expedition staying at youth hostels.*

Writing concerned with analysis can be on a wide variety of subjects, for example:

- analysing data on the increase in traffic using our roads
- analysing the significance of the witches in *Macbeth*
- analysing the best place for a family holiday.

Analysing is often about balancing facts, views, opinions, detail. This might involve an examination of evidence and opinions for and against a specific issue, or evidence which balances a range of aspects on the same issue.

Read Extract A. These paragraphs could form part of a response to an examination question such as:

> There has been a lot of debate in your area recently about how poor facilities are for young people. You have decided to join the debate by writing a balanced letter to your local newspaper which analyses the pros and cons of the council funding a skate park. Write the letter.

WHAT YOU NEED TO DO
In writing to analyse, review and comment, you need to:

'present a balanced analysis of a situation, text, issue or set of ideas taking into account a range of evidence and opinions'.

You will also need to:

'cite specific and relevant textual evidence to justify critical judgements about texts'.

from Framework for Teaching English *for Year 9*

Activity 3.1b

1 Consider the analytical detail in the first paragraph of Extract A. Complete the spider diagram:

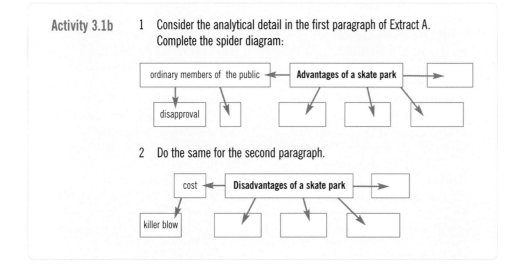

2 Do the same for the second paragraph.

The structure of a piece of analytical writing is important. If an examination question asks you to offer points of view for and against a topic, the obvious and sensible structure is four paragraphs, or sections, for example:

- **Paragraph 1: Introduction**
  Show that the topic is understood, introduce it, make general remarks.
- **Paragraph 2**
  Present points of view in favour of the issue (i.e. the advantages).
- **Paragraph 3**
  Present points of view against of the issue (i.e. the disadvantages).
- **Paragraph 4: Conclusion**
  Conclude with some open remarks.

Activity 3.1c Read Extract A again, and identify the signpost words and phrases the writer has used. (See the information in this unit.)

Notice that there are some examples of extended ideas and vocabulary in Extract A, especially towards the end of the second paragraph. Just because this is not a highly complex topic does not mean that you cannot write about it in a compelling and interesting way. Indeed you must do so.

WHAT EXAMINERS ARE LOOKING FOR

In the exam:

- at grade C: 'more selection of information for interest'; 'information likely to cover a range of aspects'
- at grade A: 'wide range of interesting information'; 'growing subtlety of purpose (to analyse) and ability to manipulate reader'

In coursework:

- at grade C: 'analyse through a structured, well expressed piece of continuous prose'
- at grade A: 'demonstrate a variety of registers and styles in analytical writing'.

In Activity 3.1b, you looked at a method of analysis which examined and weighed-up the advantages and disadvantages of a given issue. However, you may need to write in a less structured way than Extract A showed. For example, read Extract B.

Extract
B

Families rely on soaps to trigger debate

Most parents rely on the television and radio soaps to trigger discussion of 'difficult' personal subjects with their children, according to research published today by the National Family and Parenting Institute.

But the dramatists' portrayal of families bears little relation to real life and there is consistent over-representation of broken marriages and under-representation of gays, lesbians and bisexuals, the Institute said after detailed analysis of Coronation Street, EastEnders, Brookside and The Archers.

'The majority of the parents surveyed in depth for the research said that they did discuss soap stories with their families, and that soaps were helpful in bringing up issues for discussion,' it said. Two-thirds believed that storylines could help children and young people to understand about family life and 60% that soaps could show how families could support each other.

But 80% thought the soaps did not promote positive images of the family, highlighting too many scenes of sex and violence, a high level of infidelity, alcohol abuse and an overall feeling of negativity.

After analysing the programmes for a month, the researchers concluded that Coronation Street had the most highly stereotyped characters, but also showed the most positive relationships between fathers and children.

Brookside – which has just been cancelled – featured the most effective family support, and the most family crises. There was little conflict in The Archers, but EastEnders featured scenes of serious conflict throughout, which frequently erupted into physical violence.

There were many more single-parent families in the three television soaps than in real life. Only 40% of the families in EastEnders, 50% in Coronation Street and 57% in Brookside were two-parent families, compared with a British average of 74%. The equivalent figure for The Archers was 89%.

Analysis of parents' reaction was based on detailed discussion with a panel of more that 100 parents. This is the first time British soaps have been looked at from the perspective of the family and asking what the portrayal of family life is saying to parents and children.

from The Guardian, *17 October 2002*

Activity 3.1d   Extract B is a model of analysis. To analyse the article itself, answer these questions.

1 What is the topic or issue being analysed in the article?
2 Who or what is the authority which gives credibility to the analysis?
3 Explain the content and the function of the third paragraph.
4 What are the overall findings of the analysis?
5 Summarise the interesting findings of the analysis.
6 Explain in note form how the article is structured. Is it in sections? Could you improve on the arrangement of paragraphs?
7 Write down the synonyms for *analyse* which this article demonstrates.

Serious practice

UNIT ACTIVITY 3.1   You have been asked to evaluate the benefits and pitfalls of credit cards, with the possibility that young people over 16 will be able to own and use them. Write your analysis as an article aimed at those young people, using the source material below.

CREDIT CARDS	
Advantages	**Disadvantages**
• Goods can be purchased quickly and easily, in person, over the phone or on-line.	• If you fail to repay your borrowings within the grace period, credit cards tend to be expensive and are hard to control
• Credit cards are international and can be used all over the world, wherever you see the logo on your card.	• Other forms of borrowing can prove cheaper, for example, a personal loan or extension of your existing mortgage. These options should be considered before applying for a credit card.
• Credit cards can provide you with a cost-free form of finance – as long as you repay the money within the grace period.	• It is advisable to keep your receipts of purchases made. Mistakes do happen and you should cross-check your receipts with your monthly statement. Any discrepancies should be reported immediately to the company.
• Some credit cards offer perks such as discount vouchers, Air Miles and even cash-back on purchases.	• Purchases made abroad may not appear on your statement for a few months and it is therefore difficult to control.
• Some companies offer insurance on your purchases, and can protect your goods in the event of loss or theft. They can also provide you with travel insurance.	• Your credit card may be stolen or lost which produces considerable inconvenience.
• Credit cards can provide you with instant access to cash (for which there is usually a fee payable).	

Hints

◈ Read the question carefully. Identify the words which refer to the purpose, the audience and the form of the writing.
◈ You need to:

- use the source material given below, or some of it, in a brainstorm
- structure your answer into clear paragraphs or sections
- use signpost words and phrases
- develop the detail into readable continuous prose
- use stylistic devices
- use an interesting, extended vocabulary.

STYLE
It is important to write stylishly. Use rhetorical and structural features to enhance your writing.

TONE
Decide upon an appropriate tone. Since analysis is not argument, the tone should be neutral, subtle, showing nuance, rather than extreme or excessive.

VOCABULARY
You should use a developed vocabulary, imagery and diction. You are trying to impress a marker or examiner, so write vividly. Look at how Extract B uses a metaphor to good effect in the title.

Unit 3.2

Writing to review

The unit activity is to write different types of review (see page 109).

Extract
A

It would be wrong to say that this Harry Potter movie lacks magic. It is in effect all magic, but of the Magicians' Circle variety. The true absence is wonder, as well as surprise. The mysterious gothic beauty of Hogwarts, as first encountered and explored in *Harry Potter and the Philosopher's Stone*, is now familiar. So the movie concentrates upon special effects which tend to swamp the narrative.

Not that there is much of a tale here, and certainly nothing particularly resonant – just something about a terrible force contained in a secret chamber that was built in some dark recess of the school 50 years ago by an agent of the malevolent fallen angel, Voldemort.

Nevertheless the special effects are impressive. One of the effects sequences, in which a marvelously insouciant Miriam Margolyes as Professor Sprout hands out ear-muffs to her pupils while instructing them in the making of mandrake potions, is gruesomely funny. A couple of others are truly frightening – Harry and Ron surrounded in the Forbidden Forest by large carnivorous spiders and Harry battling in a sewer with a giant basilisk, wielding his magical sword like Siegfried.

Possibly the oddest aspect of the tale is the prominence given to that alluring taboo place, the girls' lavatory, used as a secret rendezvous by Harry, Ron and Hermione. An old Victorian style loo wreathed in cobwebs, it's no longer frequented because many years ago a sad, self-pitying girl nicknamed Moaning Myrtle was killed there and her ghost haunts the cubicles. The ultimate way to the secret chamber and its sinuous occupant is located here. You hardly need Sigmund Freud to explicate this.

But don't let's get too serious. This film is a lot of fun, and only adults with their limited attention spans will find it too long – which in fact it is.

adapted from The Observer, *17 November 2002*

Making a start

Writing to review is one of the most popular purposes for writing. There are many examples of reviewing:

- The most obvious are probably film reviews, book reviews and record reviews. These are found in dedicated magazines and in newspapers on a daily basis.
- There are also radio and television programmes devoted to reviews of stage, screen and print.
- Travel destinations are assessed as a form of advertising, fashion designs are discussed, cars are test-driven – all of these activities, most of which require writing, are reviews.

There are other kinds of reviewing too, for example:

- Social issues are reviewed, such as the efficiency of our hospital services.
- You may review your school's rules on uniform.
- Government policy is reviewed.
- You may look back at an event, or series of events, and evaluate their effect.

This is reviewing in the more literal sense of re-viewing – looking again at something.

Reviewing incorporates elements of analysis and of forming opinion. Here are some words and phrases which mean the same as *review*:

- *evaluate*
- *criticise*
- *discuss*
- *give one's opinion of*

- *write a critique of*
- *re-assess*
- *re-consider*
- *revise.*

Extract A is a review of the film *Harry Potter and the Chamber of Secrets*. It is a conventional film review and the activities in which the writer has engaged are criticise, discuss, give one's opinion of, write a critique of.

WHAT YOU NEED TO DO
In writing to analyse, review and comment, you need to be able to:

- 'reflect on the nature and significance of the subject matter
- form your own views, taking into account a range of evidence and opinions
- organise your ideas and information, distinguishing between analysis and comment.'

from The National Curriculum for English

Activity 3.2a   Read Extract A and answer these questions.

1   List the opinions the writer has of the film. You could quote directly or paraphrase what he says.
2   How many negative and how many positive things does the writer say about the film?
3   What is the focus of the review? Perhaps there is more than one?
4   Comment on the balance of the review.
5   How do you know that this review is intended for wide readership, including well-read adults?
6   How would you describe the tone and diction of the review?
7   Look at the three aspects quoted from the National Curriculum for this type of writing above. Does this review comply with these?

Read Extract B (page 108). This is an interesting text since it is a review of a Government review! The Government think tank in its review has *re-assessed*, *revised* and *re-considered* energy policy and, in this review of the review, the pressure group Friends of the Earth are *criticising* it. The pressure group are offering comments on the review; you could also say that they are analysing the main findings of the review. Note that the article is structured and focused – certain aspects of the think tank's work have evidently been selected for criticism.

Extract B

A Government think tank – the Performance and Innovation Unit – has just published its long-awaited energy review. The review will form the basis of an Energy White Paper that will set the agenda for Britain's energy policy for the next 50 years.

What does the Energy Review say?
Most worryingly the report recommends keeping open the option of building new nuclear power stations. Friends of the Earth is working hard to ensure that the Government does not give in to pressure from the nuclear industry.

The report extends the target for renewables [for example, energy from the sun, sea and wind] to 20 per cent by 2020. This is low given the massive potential for renewable energy in the UK. Scotland alone has the potential to supply 30 per cent of the UK's energy supply from renewables. The UK also has the largest wind resources of any European country.

Despite the large environmental impacts of coal burning, the emissions in the UK from coal burning are on the increase. Yet the report resists the idea of European Union regulations that would decrease emissions. Friends of the Earth believe that the report should have suggested the full implementation of these regulations.

The report has strong recommendations on energy efficiency. However, the targets are little more than those that were previously proposed in 1995.

adapted from
http://www.foe.co.uk/campaigns/clim
ate/news/energy_review

Activity 3.2b

1 Copy this table and complete it for Extract B:

What the think tank review said	What Friends of the Earth said

2 How does the writer of Extract B make clear that it is a review?
3 Does the writer achieve balance?
4 Is Extract A more balanced than Extract B? Explain your answer.

REVIEW, ANALYSIS AND BALANCE
Analytical writing is essentially balanced and detached, but review need not be.

It is possible for a review to be slating, censorious, lambasting, super-critical. If done well, with vivid and extended vocabulary, allusion and imagery, such writing may be highly amusing and successful.

KEY WORDS
Critic, critical, criticise and *critique* are used particularly in connection with reviewing.

critical
To be critical usually means to be disparaging, against, disapproving, fault-finding, negative. But in the context of writing discursively, it does not mean these things alone, rather it means to be accurate, diagnostic, discerning, perceptive, precise.

criticise
To use these wider techniques in an essay or article.

critique
An essay, article or some other form of writing, which uses a critical technique.

critic
The person who does the writing.

The use of language

The writer of Extract B presents a point of view – he or she has a critical standpoint in relation to the Government's view of energy provision. The review of the Government proposals reflects this – the writer is more 'critical' in the disparaging sense of the word.

Activity 3.2c List the words which are intended to guide the reader's thinking in this direction, the first such word is *worryingly*, although the fact that the review has been *long awaited* might indicate that someone has been reluctant to release it.

Find some more examples of words and phrases which are 'loaded' rather than neutral.

Serious practice

Here are two types of review task which you might be asked to undertake:

- 1 may be accomplished in a short time span since it requires planning and thinking rather than research
- 2a and 2b would be more suited to coursework.

UNIT ACTIVITY 3.2

1 You have been asked to review a book or film which you have recently enjoyed. Your review article will appear on the school's website for parents and students to enjoy.

2 a) In a few year's time, you may no longer have to go on your annual holiday with your parents – in fact you may not be asked! Think back to some of the good times you have had, remind yourself of them; re-assess them and review the good and bad times in an essay.

   b) Choose a topic of interest to you – local or world news, sport or entertainment. Carry out some research into the major events of the past year and write a critical review of some of the achievements and failures.

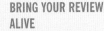

BRING YOUR REVIEW ALIVE
You need to be able to use a thesaurus to enhance diction and bring your review alive.

A weak use of language would be to say that:

- the narrative (plot) of the book was *exciting*, or that it was *boring*
- the characters were *believable* – or not
- the language was *good* or *emotional*.

A thesaurus will help you to find more interesting alternatives to these words:

exciting
exhilarating, inspiring, moving, rip-roaring, thrilling, gripping, …

boring
dull, humdrum, lacklustre, tedious, flat, wearisome, long-winded, monotonous, repetitive, slow-moving, …

believable
authentic, credible, plausible, imaginable, lively, touchable, …

good
vivid, imaginative, colourful, alive, compelling, engaging, extended, …

emotional
passionate, sensitive, tender, poignant, stirring, tear-jerking, ardent, …

Hints

- Read the questions carefully. Identify the words which refer to the purpose, the audience and the form of the writing.
- You might use a table like this to plan your book or film review:

Focus of review	Positive aspects	Negative aspects
Setting and time		
Characterisation		
Narrative		
Language		
Best parts		
Worst parts		

You might transfer your ideas from here to a spider diagram where you can collect interesting words and phrases for each section of the review.

- Use these positive categories which might prompt you to look again at (i.e. to review) past holidays with your parents:

Unit 3.3

Writing to comment

The unit activity is to write an essay and a speech which comment (see page 113).

Extract A

GORDON STRACHAN comments on being an international manager

At one time, most club managers would have loved the chance to work at international level, but this is not so much the case now and certainly not with me. At the risk of prompting the suggestion that I should be so lucky, I would not like to be in charge of a national team and I find it difficult to visualise myself having a change of attitude, especially while working in the Premiership.

One reason is the extent to which the increase in the number of small countries has affected the overall standard of international football. For much of the time I was involved as a Scotland player, matches represented a step-up from most league games. Now, they are often a step down. This particularly applies to those earning their living in the Premiership.

from The Observer, *16 February 2003*

Extract B

When Henry Olonga and Andrew Flower took to the field for Zimbabwe's opening World Cup cricket match wearing black armbands, having issued a statement which deplored 'the death of democracy in our beloved Zimbabwe' and called for an end to human-rights abuses, they showed little concern for the risks they were taking with their careers, their personal safety and even their lives. There, and in Olonga's interview with *The Observer* today, we see a clarity and courage depressingly absent from the manoeuverings and mixed motives over morality, politics, safety and television money which dominated the saga of England's 'Will they? Won't they?' match in Harare, finally cancelled last Wednesday.

from The Observer, *16 February 2003*

Making a start

It is possible to write an analysis without expressing a viewpoint, preference or opinion. This would be an entirely detached, descriptive piece of writing lacking imagination and is not likely to be something you are asked to do. Reviewing, as you have seen, involves critical discussion, evaluation, assessment or re-assessment. The expression of a personal point of view or stand-point is integral to this writing purpose.

Writing to comment also often requires the expression of opinion. To make a comment about an issue or event is to express *a view about it, to point out, to remark, to observe, to interpret or to judge.* The comment *could* be factual, detached and impersonal, simply adding to knowledge, but we usually expect a comment to be the expression of feeling or belief.

Similarly, a *commentator* who is commenting on a sports competition or a public event relays the events by describing what is going on, but also, often, expresses a *judgement* and an *impression*.

FORMS OF WRITING

You need to:

'analyse, review and comment, focusing on considered and evaluative views of ideas, texts and issues.

The forms of such writing should be drawn from reviews, commentaries, articles, essays, reports.'

from The National Curriculum for English, Breadth of Study section

Newspapers provide many examples of writing to analyse, review and coment. They often devote a section or supplement to *reviews* and to *comment*. The editorial, or leader column, is often a *comment* on one of the main news stories. Reader's letters are also a source for comments.

Activity 3.3a   Write out the key words from the paragraphs above which identify comment.

Extract A is a good example of a personal standpoint being expressed largely as assertions.

Activity 3.3b
1   List Gordon Strachan's comments in Extract A.
2   Which of his comments are assertions?
3   Do you think the points are made clearly and effectively? Why?

Extract B is an example of a comment on a sporting event in newspaper's leader column. There is information in the text and description, but the leader writer's main purpose is to make a comment, assert an opinion, share his impression of the event and his judgement of it.

Activity 3.3c   Read Extract B.
1   Write down the comments which are the focus of the text.
2   Which comment(s) are assertions and which would you call judgements?
      Use your own words and quotations to support your answer.

Extract C on page 112 is less straightforward. Read it carefully – there is more than one level of comment in it.

Activity 3.3d
1   Who is the subject of the writer's comments?
2   What other comments are presented in the writing?

COMMENT NOT ARGUMENT

Keep in mind that the purpose of your writing in this unit is to *comment*.

Commenting on a topic or issue is not the same as arguing for or against it. The difference is one of degree and forcefulness. You can have a point of view, a judgement, about congestion charges, based on knowledge from analysis of the issue, which is *subtle, detached, unemotional* – you are not *disputing* or *remonstrating*.

Look back at Extract A. Gordon Strachan is not arguing vehemently against being an international football manager, rather he is making a *judgement*, an *observation*, a *comment* on the issue with phrases such as 'I would find it difficult to visualise myself …'.

His point of view is all the more effective for this style of writing.

Extract C

All last week the harridans raked Catherine Zeta-Jones's pouty face with their pens.

The best that could be said for her was that she was out of touch with her Swansea roots. As for the worst that could be said… well, there was no worst. A thesaurus of words meaning greedy, vainglorious, manipulative and insensitive was poured upon the Oscar nominee's raven-tressed head. It was wrong, terribly wrong of her to sue *Hello!* magazine for half a million, just because they gate crashed her New York wedding, took a few unauthorised snaps, and then chartered a special jet to fly copies of *Hello!* to British newsstands before the official pics could appear in the rival *OK!* magazine.

Interestingly, it seems to have been understood from the start that it is Zeta-Jones who is the villain here. It was her appearance in the witness box last Monday that provoked the most acid to be secreted from the deep ducts of Britain's red-top columnesses.

from The Observer, *16 February 2003*

Tone, diction and voice

Extracts A, B and C are all successful pieces of writing, but they differ in tone, diction and voice.

Activity 3.3e

1 Look back to page 71 and decide which tone words listed there best apply to each of the extracts in this unit.
2 Comment on the use of diction (vocabulary) in the texts. Which is the most colourful and engaging?
3 The inclusion or exclusion of the persona of the writer is a factor in the extracts. In which extract is the writer most obviously involved and in which one is the writer least involved?
4 Discuss which extract(s) you preferred. Which impressed you most and why?

Serious practice

UNIT ACTIVITY 3.3   Coursework assignment

1 **Paying to use your car**
Within the next few years it is possible that you will be required to pay road toll charges for using some motorways and congestion charges to take your car into the centre of cities.

Write an essay which interprets the implications of these proposals and comment on the effect you think they will have.

continued

Hints

◆ Read the questions carefully. Identify the words which refer to the purpose, the audience and the form of the writing.
◆ Consider the ideas in *Planning your work*.

UNIT ACTIVITY 3.3 **Examination question**
(continued)

2   There is a proposal in your school to change the school day. Lessons will be taught between 8.30 a.m. and 5.30 p.m.; you will have lessons within these times. Some days you may not start lessons until 10.30 a.m., other days you may not finish until 5.30 p.m. You will have free time for study in the library. There is to be an open forum on the subject.

Write the text of a speech which includes your comments on the subject. You intend to make the speech at the meeting.

Planning your work

Question 1: gathering ideas

- You will need to do some research. Typing 'congestion charges' and 'motorway tolls UK' into a search engine will produce lots of basic detail to work with.
- Remember the focus of the assignment is not information or description but *comment*. You are bound to include information, description and some analysis, just as Extract A, B and C did, but the focus is on:
  - your *point of view* – where you stand on the issue
  - your *judgement* as to the effects/outcomes
  - your *impression* of the effect on people
  - any *observations* you wish to make.
- This spider diagram summarises the issues you need to comment upon:

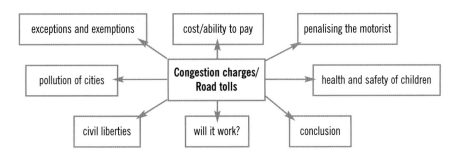

Question 2: possible paragraph plan

- **Paragraph 1: Introduction** Show that the topic is understood – elaborate on the ideas behind a flexible day. Show that there are pros and cons to the idea.
- **Paragraph 2:** Develop the detail of the issue with some examples of the implications, perhaps anecdotal, speculative, 'What if …' points. Make judgements, observations, comments on these.
- **Paragraph 3:** Widen the issue to more general comments – safety of children late home, extending the workload of teachers, the effect on the family, the added responsibility of students dealing with study time, etc.
- **Paragraph 4: Conclusion** Make a rounded conclusion which focuses on your audience. You do not need a definitive answer – a witty comment to end with would be good.

 WRITING THE TEXT OF A SPEECH

This is a form of writing which you may practise, not only for examination preparation, but also for Speaking and Listening tasks for coursework.

Question 2 of the unit activity is a writing exercise, so you should use *standard English*.

It should be *well-structured*, so that your *comments* are clear and easy to follow to their conclusion.

You should take the opportunity to focus on your *audience*, reminding the marker or examiner that you have the 'speech' element of the task in mind.

Use signpost words and phrases which are *inclusive* (i.e. they include the audience in the speech), for example:

- *I'm sure you will agree that …*
- *You will have noticed that …*
- *Imagine the situation when you …*
- *How many times have you thought that ….*

But remember, as with all linguistic features, do not overdo it – try to avoid cliché.

Unit 3.4

Establishing a relationship with your reader

The unit activity is to analyse and comment on the readership of two newspapers (see page 117).

COMMENT

• •

We must act to end the sweatshops

Your campaign against the exploitation of Third World workers in the fashion industry brings to mind my first experience of seeing real sweatshops. This was in an industrial area of Hong Kong in 1987. 'Made in Hong Kong' was a label that was becoming more and more popular, and I was curious to see what lay behind it. The place felt like hell on earth. The colour of the air was different from anywhere else in Hong Kong. The dye and oil coming from the machines was left to drift into the streets, and it gave the whole area a black and slippery quality. Many of the workers slept in the factories, some of them under their machines. I found all this incredibly disturbing, yet the workers seemed grateful to have a roof over their heads and something to do. I was amazed at their acceptance of their conditions.

For my part, I had started out as a fashion designer in the early 1980s. My clothes were made in the East End of London. The factories I used weren't sweatshops, but they were about as near as you could get to it. I didn't know what the girls were getting paid, but I'm certain it wasn't very much. The first factory I worked with was a part-funded government scheme, set up because it had been given start-up support, and it was literally a hand-to-mouth existence. The business lived from one order to the next. The factories making leather goods looked as if they had not moved on since Dickensian times.

from The Independent, *25 September 1999*

Making a start

You need to be clear who you are writing for. If you have an audience in mind, you will find it easier to decide on the detail of your writing and the tone, diction and style you should use.

Let us take the coursework assignment suggested on the right as an example. The task includes the idea of sending the report to the BBC and ITV. This audience is not, therefore, the same as if you were writing something light-hearted for your school magazine, or complaining about TV programmes to your local newspaper. The tone of the assignment would need to be

- serious
- thoughtful
- sincere
- authoritative.

Its *analytical* content would need to be:

- accurate
- dependable
- factual
- balanced
- detailed.

As with other writing purposes, there are a number of things to consider when thinking about the audience for whom the writing is intended:

- What is or is not the intended age range?
- Is the audience specific?
- What is the level of language ability assumed?
- How does the style fit the audience?
- How specialised is the audience?
- Is the audience in a particular context?

QUESTIONS WITH COMBINED PURPOSES

In Units 3.1–3.3 you thought about and practised writing to analyse, review and comment. You may be set a coursework assignment or exam question which focuses on one element alone as the practice questions did in these units. Or they may be combined.

Here are two examples of questions which combine more than one purpose for writing:

- For examination practice:

  Young people have had mobile phones for some years now and the demand for them has not decreased.

  Write an account for your school magazine which analyses the use, misuse and hazards of students owning mobile phones and comment on whether or not they should be allowed in school.

- For a coursework assignment:

  Not Real-Life Drama!
  It has been claimed that television portrays either open violence, verbal violence, violence dressed up as comedy or is just downright depressing and traumatic – and all before the watershed.

  Analyse the programming on BBC1 and ITV for a period of time with this issue in mind. Review what other people of your age think and comment on your findings.

  You will send your report to the two broadcasting companies concerned.

Activity 3.4a

1 Think of some words which you should keep in mind when brainstorming your material for the *review* and *comment* parts of the assignment.
2 What tone would the writing have if the assignment was:
   a) an article for the school magazine?
   b) a letter complaining to the local press?

Activity 3.4b

Read the review of *Harry Potter and the Chamber of Secrets* again (Extract A, page 106). The review appeared in *The Observer*. Although the film's target audience is children or young people, the review ranges wider than this for its readership.

1 Answer the questions listed above in relation to the review.
2 What do you think the following phrases mean?
   a) 'the Magicians' Circle variety'
   b) 'mysterious gothic beauty'
   c) 'swamp the narrative'
   d) 'nothing particularly resonant'
   e) 'insouciant'
   f) 'magical sword like Siegfried'
   g) 'You hardly need Sigmund Freud to expiate this'
3 a) What do you think the writer is getting at with these clever pieces of diction?
   b) Do they help the review or get in its way?

continued

DESCRIPTION

Part of the effect of the writing by Helen Storey, particularly in the first paragraph, is her power to use *descriptive words and phrases.*

Writing to describe is not part of this writing triplet (you studied it in Section 2). However, it is impossible not to describe things for most purposes. The point is that the writer's main purpose, the focus of her writing, is to *comment* on the issue.

Notice that the really engaging aspect of the writing lies in the extended use of vocabulary in the descriptive part of the extract.

WHAT EXAMINERS ARE LOOKING FOR

In the exam:

- at grade C: 'clear identification with purpose and audience'; 'begin to sustain reader response'
- at grade A: 'form, content and style are … matched to audience'

In coursework:

- at grade C: 'adapt style and form to different audiences'
- at grade A: 'writing is elaborate or concise, vigorous or restrained according to audience'.

Activity 3.4b (continued)

4 What is the intended audience?

5 How does the writer stay on side with a younger readership at the end of his review?

6 Read the information below.
   a) Which of the above phrases are allusions?
   b) Which is a metaphor?
   c) Which is just good, vivid writing?

LANGUAGE AND YOUR AUDIENCE

The level of language used in a piece of writing is often the way in which writers target particular readers.

A simple piece of writing can be understood be everyone — but the diction will be basic, uninspiring and lack development. You should try to write with a developed and extended vocabulary, especially for assessment purposes.

In the case of the Harry Potter review, most students of your age would not, perhaps, understand the references to the Magic Circle, Siegfried or Freud. But it does not stop you understanding the review as a whole. These references are called *allusions* — they are an extended and clever way of writing, if appropriate and not overdone. An allusion mentions something or someone who acts in a similar way to the subject of your topic but is nothing directly to do with it.

If you are writing a review and you want to make allusions to something you know about, then do so! You might allude to your sporting interest, a footballer, a hobby, favourite entertainer, unusual musical interest — whatever fits.

Activity 3.4c

You are going to analyse some extracts from the article above which is from the Comment section of *The Independent,* written by Helen Storey.

1 Read the article with writing to analysis, review and comment in mind. Who does the writer have in mind as her audience?

2 Answer these questions on the first paragraph:

   a) In what ways is the paragraph a review?
   b) Who does the first word 'Your' refer to? How does this engage the reader?
   c) Is there a specific audience mind, as well as a general newspaper audience? Explain your answer.
   d) How does the writer include her readers in the underlined sentence?
   e) Some analysis of conditions is hiding behind the descriptive passages. List the information you learn from the paragraph.
   f) What is the voice being used? How is it effective?
   g) What comments are made by the writer at the end of the paragraph?
   h) Explain how the content of the paragraph is deliberately structured to maximise the effect on the reader.

3 How does the second paragraph develop the comments of the first and reinforce engagement with the reader?

Serious practice

UNIT ACTIVITY 3.4 Coursework assignment

National Daily Newspapers and Their Readership: A Report
You will need to choose two different national daily newspapers. A good pair would be a broadsheet, such as *The Guardian* and a tabloid, such as the *Daily Mail* or *Daily Mirror*. Choose a random weekday.

Your task is to:

1 Research the readership of each newspaper in terms of numbers and types of reader.
2 Analyse the contents of each front page.
3 Comment on factors which seem to deliberately determine readership.

Hints

- Read the question carefully. Identify the words which refer to the purpose and the form of the writing. Read the information on this page about the audience.
- Use the table in *Gathering ideas* to structure your research.

Gathering ideas

Use the features and questions in the table below as the basis for a spider diagram or other method of brainstorm. Use also any other questions which occur to you as you undertake your initial analysis and draft.

Feature	Questions to ask
Pictures	How many pictures are there? What size are they?
	What proportion of the page are they?
	Do they dominate and lead the eye?
	What function do they have?
	Are they central/focused/relevant or decorative/sensational?
Headlines	How many are there?
	Do they dominate?
	Are they essential or sensational?
	Do they say anything?
	Are there subheadings, banners, flags, abstracts as well?
Type of story	News? Politics/Financial? Entertainment? Crime?
Number of words	Comment on the relative number of words.
	Are there more in the broadsheet?
	Are words the largest feature of the page?
Number of stories	Does one story dominate?
	Is there news in brief?
	Is there a full, developed story?
Level of diction	Are the sentences short with basic, simple vocabulary?
	What would you say was the reading age, or level, of the words used?
	Is there anything you don't understand in the tabloid?
	How about the broadsheet?
Number of concepts/ideas	Are there difficult/complicated items on the front page?
	Does everything interest you?
	How much of the broadsheet front page would you not be bothered about reading?
	How much of the tabloids?
Complexity of style	Which of the stories uses vivid, imaginative words? Images? Allusion?

YOUR AUDIENCE FOR THE UNIT ACTIVITY

Imagine you are to send your report to the market research teams at the newspapers concerned.

The *tone* of your assignment will need to be:

- serious
- thoughtful
- sincere
- authoritative.

Its *analytical* content will need to be:

- accurate
- dependable
- detailed
- supported by evidence
- factual
- balanced.

Your *comments* should be:

- perceptive
- learned
- helpful
- illuminating
- honest
- well expressed
- humorous.

Unit 3.5
Choosing the right style

The unit activity is to write an analysis and comment for the school magazine (see page 121).

Extract A

The room was too big, the ceiling was too high, the doors were too tall, and the white carpet went from wall to wall like a fresh fall of snow at Lake Arrowhead. There were full length mirrors and crystal doodads all over the place. The ivory furniture had chromium on it, and the enormous ivory drapes lay tumbled on the white carpet a yard from the windows. The white made the ivory look dirty and the ivory made the white look bled out. The windows stared towards the darkening foothills. It was going to rain soon. There was pressure in the air already.

I sat down on the edge of a deep soft chair and looked at Mrs Regan. She was worth a stare. She was trouble. She was stretched out on a modernistic chaise-longue with her slippers off, so I stared at her legs in the sheerest silk stockings. They seemed to be arranged to stare at.

from The Big Sleep *by Raymond Chandler*

Making a start

Style can be defined as:

> any specific and deliberate way of using language which characterises a **genre**, **register**, **purpose** or intention in writing.

Let us look more closely at *genre*, *register* and *purpose*.

Genre

In writing of a particular genre, you will be able to see a particular style. Look at the 'family tree' of a genre opposite: from the broad genre of *Prose*, we can narrow down to a particular style and, in fact, to a particular author, since each author has a distinctive style.

Each of the boxes below *Prose* is a **sub-genre**. Each sub-genre will demonstrate writing of a particular style. This will include the words used (**diction**), **syntax, structural features, linguistic** and **rhetorical features** and **tone**.

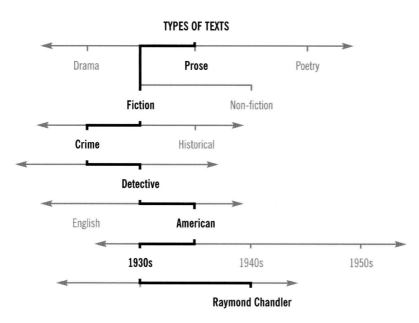

Having arrived at Raymond Chandler in the 'family tree', read Extract A which is from his book, *The Big Sleep*.

Purpose
The purpose of Chandler's writing in Extract A is essentially to describe, but also to set a tone and mood.

Register
The term *register* refers to the form of language used in particular circumstances. The circumstances in Extract A are formal, literary, fictional and descriptive.

Activity 3.5a	Read Extract A and answer these questions.

1 Chandler is setting a tone or mood. Which of the following words describes the tone or mood, do you think?

comfortable	domestic	exciting	safe
complacent	elegant	exotic	sinister
dangerous	erotic	relaxed	

2 Comment on the opening sentence of the extract. What does Chandler achieve by it?
3 Comment on Chandler's varied length of sentence.
4 How do the phrases 'going to rain', 'pressure in the air' and 'on the edge' reflect the tone of the writing?
5 Find and comment on the imagery and alliteration which Chandler uses.
6 Would you say that there was an ironic tone to the extract, as if Chandler had his tongue in his cheek? Explain your answer.

Style is no less a factor in non-fiction writing to analyse, review and comment. For example, read Extract B.

Extract B

ANALYSIS

WHAT A WASTE

Plans to use recycling, composting and incineration to reduce the amount of rubbish we throw into holes in the ground are in deep trouble.

The United Kingdom has a bad record in dealing with its rubbish compared with other European countries. In the 90s, international pressure stopped the dumping of chemical and sewage waste directly into the North sea, a practice that had led the UK under Mrs Thatcher to be dubbed the 'dirty man of Europe'. On land, nothing has changed.

While Germany, Denmark and the Netherlands forge ahead with recycling, composting and using waste to generate energy, the UK carries on dumping in landfill sites. The result is that this country is years behind the best in Europe in dealing with the growing mountain of domestic and commercial waste. And we are failing to gain the new industries and jobs that active recycling of rubbish brings.

The explanation is lack of political will both at national and local level and an easy option – lots of big holes of the ground. In the UK at the end of last year only 8% of waste was recycled, 8% burned to make electricity and – in a nation of gardeners – only 1% composted to improve the soil. This left 83% simply being dumped in holes.

Pressure on the UK has come from a series of European Union directives intended to restrict use of excessive packaging and so cut the ever-climbing amounts of waste a consumer society throws away. To comply with the latest EU landfill directive the government has set new targets for recovering and recycling materials. More waste has to be converted into energy. By 2005, 40% of waste must be recovered or burned. The target for 2010 is 45% and 67% by 2015.

Meanwhile, the other main plank of official policy, incineration, is in deep trouble. The idea of reducing waste bulk by burning it while at the same time generating electricity is appealing. The problem in the UK is that there has been successful and continuing opposition that may veto any expansion.

from The Guardian, 11 October 2000

SOME ELEMENTS OF STYLE

diction
The words, phrases, images employed by the writer.

syntax
The arrangement of the words in grammatical sentences — short, long, varied.

imagery
The use of simile, metaphor and personification to make the writing vivid and engaging.

linguistic features
Puns, rhetorical questions, lists, ironic statements, exaggeration …

structural features
The organisation of paragraphs, indentation, bullet points, length of sentences, headings, subheadings, abstracts to make the sense clear.

There are a number of things to be said about the style and tone of Extract B. It:

- is formally written in standard English
- is based on detached, objective analysis
- has a historical dimension
- presents supporting statistics
- contains detailed material
- presents impression, judgements, observations rather than forceful argument
- remains open-ended.

On closer analysis, however, there are quite a few other things going on stylistically.

Activity 3.5b   Remind yourself of the elements of style above. Then answer these questions on Extract B.

1   Explain the writer's use of puns.
2   Comment on the writer's use of lists.
3   Comment on the writer's use of connectives.
4   Find and explain the writer's use of imagery in the text.
5   Does the writer use repetition deliberately? Where?
6   Where is assertion used in the first paragraph?
7   Write down the sentences in the text which are truly analytical and detached, and those which are comment – assertion, opinion. Comment on your findings.
8   Choose another word for *bad* in the first line of the second paragraph.
9   Choose a sentence and rewrite it as a rhetorical question.

A good way to understand and experience a writer's style is to **parody** his or her writing (see right).

Activity 3.5c
1 Remind yourself of the work you did on Extract A. Write a short description of a room and a person in it which parodies Chandler's style of writing.
2 Look back at the Helen Storey extract in Unit 3.4 where she reviews her time in Hong Kong. Write a paragraph which revisits a place you know which is unpleasant and squalid. Use the same voice, tone and use of imagery as Helen Storey does.

Serious practice

UNIT ACTIVITY 3.5 **Examination question**
There has been concern expressed about the amount of litter and waste which is generated by your community. You have noticed this, particularly in your own school environment.
Analyse the extent of the problem and comment on possible solutions in an essay for your school magazine.

Hints

◆ Read the question carefully. Identify the words which refer to the purpose, the audience and the form of the writing.
◆ Focus on the tone and style of your writing.

◆ Use the words and phrases in the spider diagram below as a reminder of the features of style. Ensure that they are included in your essay.

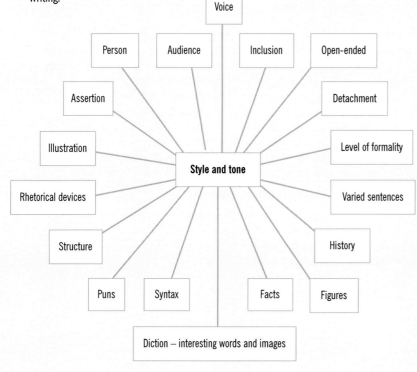

Voice
Person Audience Inclusion Open-ended
Assertion Detachment
Illustration Level of formality
Rhetorical devices — **Style and tone** — Varied sentences
Structure History
Puns Syntax Facts Figures
Diction – interesting words and images

PARODY
A parody is, in effect, the copying of a writer's style. The dictionary says it is:

composition in which an author's characteristics are humorously imitated.

Some synonyms for *parody* are:
◆ *caricature*
◆ *imitate*
◆ *mimic*
◆ *send-up*
◆ *satirise.*

ACCURACY
Your writing, however stylish it may be, must be accurate.

Here are some criteria for accuracy which examiners use at the top level:

◆ Use complex grammatical structures and punctuation with success.
◆ Organise writing using sentence demarcation (punctuation).
◆ Employ a variety of sentence forms to good effect.
◆ Show accuracy in the spelling of words from an ambitious vocabulary.
◆ Use standard English appropriately.

Unit 3.6

Forms of writing

The unit activity is to write a magazine article which analyses and comments (see page 125).

Extract
A

NEWS COMMENTARY

UK Stewart Report into Mobile Phones and Health

In 1999 the UK Government established an independent expert group (IEGMP), headed by Sir William Stewart, to examine possible health effects of mobile phones, base stations and transmitters on health.

The Independent Expert Group on Mobile Phones (IEGMP) released the report on Mobile Phones and Health on 11 May 2000.

The report adopted a precautionary approach and made numerous recommendations. The most significant of which are outlined below.

Summary of the More Significant IEGMP Assessment's of Health Risks from the Mobile Phone System

The Stewart Group has concluded that the balance of evidence suggests that for mobile phone users:

> *exposure to radio-frequency radiation below guideline levels does not cause adverse health effects to the general public.*

However, the Stewart Group has also concluded that there is now scientific evidence that:

> *there may be biological effects occurring at exposures below these guidelines. This does not necessarily mean that these effects lead to disease or injury but this is important information.*

The Stewart Group concluded that:

> *it is not possible at present to say that exposure to RF radiation, even at levels below national guidelines, is totally without potential adverse health effects, and that the gaps in knowledge are sufficient to justify a precautionary approach.*

Drivers

The Stewart Group further concluded in relation to the risks of mobile phones:

> *that their use in cars can increase the chance of accidents and that*

> *drivers should be dissuaded from using phones on the move.*

Children

The Stewart Group stated that it believes that the widespread use of mobile phones by children for non-essential calls should be discouraged because:

> *if there are currently unrecognized adverse health effects from the use of mobile phones, children may be more vulnerable because of their developing nervous system, the greater absorption of energy in the tissues of the head and a longer lifetime of exposure.*

from http://www.arpansa.gov.au/news/stewart.htm

Making a start

Often the question in the exam, or for coursework, asks for a particular **form** of writing, for example:

* *Write a letter to a newspaper …*
* *Write an article commenting …*
* *Write an analytical report ….*

You have written in a variety of forms already in this section: an article, an essay, the text of a speech, a report – all to analyse, review and comment.

The National Curriculum lists a range of forms which should be covered in writing to analyse, review and comment: 'reviews, commentaries, articles, essays and reports'. You might also be asked to write a leaflet or a letter.

Activity 3.6a

Read Extract A. It is a commentary on a report, and also contains analysis and review. Answer the following questions about it.

1. Form
    a) Explain how the text is a commentary.
    b) What other form of writing is referred to in the text?
    c) Describe the structural features of the commentary (see the information on this page).
    d) How do the structural features help your understanding of the text?
    e) How might the structural features have been enhanced?
    f) In what physical form might this commentary appear, for example, letter, leaflet, web page, newspaper report?

2. Audience
    a) Who is this commentary written for?
    b) What is or is not the intended age range?
    c) Is the audience specific?
    d) What is the level of language ability assumed?
    e) How does the style fit the audience
    f) How specialised is the audience?
    g) Is the audience in a particular context?

3. Purpose
    a) Explain in what sense this text is a review.
    b) Find and quote four statements which either are analysis or derive from analysis.
    c) Find and quote four comments from the text.

PURPOSE, FORM AND AUDIENCE

Remember that there are three elements to writing: purpose, form and audience. They are interdependent, for example, the form depends on the writer's purpose and intended audience.

As you read Extract A, think about its function in terms of:

* form
* purpose
* audience
* content
* style.

USEFUL WORDS

comment
an explanatory note, remark, criticism.

commentary
an expository treatise (setting ideas out), a series of comments on a book or remarks on an event.

* A commentary on a past event also highlights the main points, for example, a commentary on a cricket match.
* A review is also selective in bringing forth (exposing) the main points of a play, a book, a record or an event.

FEATURES OF COMMENTARY

You need to consider these structural and presentational features:

* headline/titles
* sub-titles
* length of paragraphs
* length of sentence
* organisation of sections
* indentation
* bullet points
* different fonts
* pictures, graphics, colour
* position of topic sentences
* use of key words
* spacing on the page.

You should name the form in which you are writing for each writing task you do. Here are some examples of linking a task to a form:

1 An **account** of my time at primary School.
2 A **leaflet** which analyses the different ways there are to stop smoking.
3 A **summary** of what my Saturday job entails.
4 A piece of writing which reviews the success of a recent camping and walking weekend.
5 A **leaflet** about a local beauty spot for tourists.
6 A **speech** which comments on the problems of inner city poverty.
7 A half-time **summary** of a football match for local radio.
8 An **account** of the interesting parts of my work experience week.
9 A **pamphlet** promoting recycling or vegetarianism.
10 A **record** of a sailing trip or tour of North Wales.
11 A **letter** asking a friend to stay.
12 An **article** for my local newspaper analysing the benefits of providing more facilities for young people.

ARTICLE
The dictionary defines an article as 'literary composition (other than fiction)'. So there is scope for well-crafted expression and an extended vocabulary.

COMMENTARY
A commentary includes the skill of summarising things which have been written, viewed or experienced elsewhere.

Activity 3.6b

1 Suggest a purpose (analyse, review or comment) for the writing in examples 1, 3, 5, 7, 8, 9, 10, 11 just as there is for 2, 4, 6, and 12. There can be more than one purpose.
2 Make up titles of your own for the following forms of writing, which would fit writing to analyse, review and comment:

a) prospectus   d) report
b) article   e) account.
c) letter

Serious practice

UNIT ACTIVITY 3.6 Coursework assignment

The anti-smoking pressure group ASH states that 'Giving up smoking is the one of single most beneficial things you can do for your immediate and long-term health.'

Write an article for a popular magazine read by your age group which analyses the effects of smoking on health and the influence advertising has on students of your age.

You should go on to comment on the various ways of giving up smoking suggested by ASH.

Hints

- The commentary on the various ways ASH suggests people might give up smoking is a similar task to the mobile phones commentary on page 122.
- Use the ideas and source material suggested in *Planning your writing* below.

Planning your writing

A coursework assignment allows you plenty of time to research and plan your work.

Gathering ideas

Begin to make notes on the assignment by responding to these prompts:

- Note who is your audience.
- Note that you will be analysing, reviewing and commenting at points in the assignment.

- Note that you are writing an article, then going on to write a commentary.
- Choose your tone and style.
- List some structural and linguistic devices and a developed vocabulary you might use.

Use these sources for material:

- Browse the ASH website and other websites concerned with giving up smoking or the effects of smoking.
- Interview a cross-section of smokers and non-smokers about the dangers they know of or have experienced.
- Interview people of your own age about the influence cigarette advertising has had on them.
- Find examples of advertising which you would suggest are seductive to young people.

Extract **B**

Unfortunately the insidious nature of nicotine addiction makes giving up smoking one of the most difficult things to do. In fact, the Royal College of Physicians in a report concluded that nicotine is as addictive as drugs such as heroin and cocaine.But that does not mean that you can't beat cigarettes.
On this page we'll provde you with all the informatin we can to get you started on stopping.

From http://www.ash.org.uk

Extract **C**

Quitting smoking

Q   *What's the best way to stop smoking?*
Q   *What is nicotine replacement therapy?*
Q   *How does Zyban work and is it safe?*
Q   *Will hypnotherapy and acupuncture help me to quit?*
Q   *Is it a good idea to cut down gradually before finally quitting?*

These questions are answered on the ASH website: www.ash.org.uk

---

Paragraph plan

Plan the article carefully. Include all of the key aspects of the assignment task. Focus particularly on the forms of writing. Your plan might look like this:

- **Paragraph 1: Introduction**
  Show that the topic is understood: what the issues are, what the assignment deals with and what is its structure.
- **Paragraph 2: Analyse the effects of smoking**
  Use source material, interviews, data. Present a balanced, detached view. Observe, evaluate, make judgements. Write an article.
- **Paragraph 3: Review the effects of advertising**
  Review what is happening, changes in law. Note the limitations, report on findings, look at some techniques used. Review the effect on your peers. Continue as an article.
- **Paragraph 4: Comment**
  Summarise and evaluate methods of giving up. Express a view, point out difficulties, make remarks. Write a commentary.
- **Paragraph 5: Conclusion**
  Make a rounded conclusion which focuses on your audience. You do not need a definitive answer.

WHAT EXAMINERS ARE LOOKING FOR

In the exam:

- at grade C: 'a formal article, the tone of which is appropriately balanced'
- at grade A: 'a formal letter, the tone of which is appropriately serious'

In coursework:

- at grade C: 'adapt forms to different audiences and purposes'
- at grade A: 'a variety of writing forms such as the journalistic article or revelatory letter'.

Unit 3.7

Planning your writing

The unit activity is to practise a four-paragraph structure for analytical writing (see page 129).

All teenagers to be forced to do community work

Ministers are to compel the 3 million pupils in state secondary schools to do voluntary work from next year as part of the government's mission to halt the drift to a 'selfish and soulless' society.

Children from the age of 11 will have to spend time helping others in ways such as cleaning out ponds or improving communal playgrounds as part of the citizenship programmes that all secondary schools will be required to provide.

Jan Newton, the government's newly appointed adviser on citizenship, accepted that schools would find it difficult to supervise the increased amount of voluntary work. 'We are not telling them how it is to be done or how much time is to be spent doing it. But every child will have to do it. There are ways it can be done in school, but older children helping others to read or by inviting groups into the school,' she said.

While the move was welcomed

this week by voluntary groups, it faces resistance from teaching unions. Head teachers are also sceptical. The head teacher of a Winchester school said: 'Secondary teachers are exhausted with initiatives. Who is going to organise all these activities?'

The response from schools will disappoint ministers. Citizenship lessons have come under fire from the former chief inspector of schools, who

described them as 'demoralising claptrap'. Japan, with one of the most academically competitive systems in the world, has introduced community service for all ages as part of a new moral education.

adapted from The Sunday Times, *11 July 2001*

Making a start

Throughout this book the importance of effective planning has been stressed. Whether you are writing for coursework or for examination, the same basic principles of planning apply:

- generate ideas by brainstorming or mind-mapping
- organise those ideas into a convincing piece of writing.

The stages of planning

Remember the essential techniques:

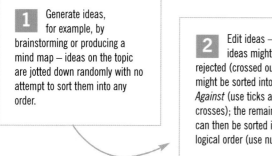

1 Generate ideas, for example, by brainstorming or producing a mind map – ideas on the topic are jotted down randomly with no attempt to sort them into any order.

2 Edit ideas – Some ideas might be rejected (crossed out); others might be sorted into *For* or *Against* (use ticks and crosses); the remaining ideas can then be sorted into a logical order (use numbers).

3 Produce a paragraph plan – arrange the numbering points into paragraphs, usualy between four and six.

What planning techniques are effective for writing to analyse, review and comment?

Writing to analyse, review or comment is generally a *balanced* type of writing. You are usually considering a topic from all angles, often in a detached, impersonal way. You may, of course, be expressing views as well, but you are not giving a passionate, one-sided argument as you might if you were writing a persuasive speech.

So balance, fairness, a cool consideration of all the issues and angles: this is what characterises writing to analyse, review and comment. Your planning, then, should reflect this need to show all sides.

A simple four-paragraph plan will ensure that you give both sides of an issue. For example, let's take a typical task:

> The town council has published a proposal to redevelop a town-centre site as a multi-storey car park. Write an analytical report on the proposal for the council.

A four-paragraph plan for the question might look like this:

- **Paragraph 1**: Introduce the topic
- **Paragraph 2**: Ideas in favour of the proposal
- **Paragraph 3**: Ideas against the proposal
- **Paragraph 4**: A conclusion which weighs up the ideas in a balanced way.

Here are some facts and opinions which you might use in an analytical report for the council:

- Existing car parks are full by 10.00 a.m.
- Surveys show that people do not like park-and-ride schemes because they have to carry their shopping too far.
- A new out-of-town shopping mall with lots of parking space will make the proposed car park unnecessary within two years.
- A town-centre car park will simply encourage car use with all its environmental problems of pollution and congestion.
- Without the new car park, the town centre could gradually die. People will go to other towns. Some shops have already closed.
- Surveys of shoppers show that younger shoppers are starting to shop in other towns.
- The proposed car park will be an eyesore in the heart of the old town.
- Most of it will be underground; it will not be visually intrusive.

WHAT EXAMINERS ARE LOOKING FOR
One of the qualities which examiners look for in an effective answer is 'a range of well-controlled sentence structures'. This means varying the **length** of your sentences, and varying the **type** of sentences, for example by using subordinate clauses.

Activity 3.7a

1 a) Which of the above are facts? Which are opinions?
   b) Since this is an imaginary situation, add some facts or opinions which might be relevant to such a proposal. These might sway the arguments one way or another, or simply make the problem more difficult to resolve.

2 Write the report.

Hint

- Use ticks and crosses or other symbols to arrange the above points into *For* and *Against* arguments.
- Use the signpost words and phrases to link the ideas above into orderly paragraphs (see below).
- You have to decide on the best order for the points within each paragraph. Numbers next to the points will help you plan this.
- It is quite acceptable to use subheadings for the paragraphs in your report. For example, you might use these headings: *The proposal, Effects on local trade, The future.*

i SIGNPOST WORDS AND PHRASES

You could use some of the following words and phrases to link your ideas in a logical sequence. They tend to express balance and fairness and take a cautious approach to expressing views.

- *While it is true that other car parks are full by mid-morning …*
- *Some people were strongly opposed to the idea that …*
- *Although there was some support for …*
- *Despite some objections to the design of the subway …*
- *A thorough survey is, therefore, urgently required before any decision …*
- *An alternative approach would be to ….*

Style of an analytical report

Reports are written in an impersonal, formal, unemotional style. The writer should not be seen to be taking sides, but to be presenting the facts and the arguments in a dispassionate, neutral way. Reports draw conclusions from facts. This means that you will not be using the first person (*I*), for example:

- *I think that some shops will be forced to close if the car park is not built.*

  would be expressed in an impersonal way, such as:

  It is likely that some shops will be forced to close if the car park is not built.

- *I don't like the design of the proposed car park and I don't think it fits in with the rest of the town.*

  Strong, direct opinions such as this are likely to be expressed in a more detached, formal style, using passive verb forms, such as:

  The car park may have to be redesigned to harmonise with the architecture of the town centre.

The extract on page 126 is an example of an analytical newspaper article. Its **purpose** is to analyse one aspect of citizenship in schools: the proposal that all secondary pupils should do community work.

It is not the purpose of the journalist to comment on the proposal; her aim is to present both sides of the debate and leave the reader to arrive at a conclusion. Any opinions are reported by the journalist; they are not presented as her own views. Often they are direct quotations.

Activity 3.7b

1 Look at the sequence of paragraphs in the article. Does the writer follow roughly the four-paragraph structure on page 127?

2 What is the function of each paragraph? Does it:
- explain the issue?
- present viewpoints in favour of community work?
- present viewpoints against?
- present a balanced conclusion?

Note: It is a common feature of journalistic writing to have short paragraphs which break up the text. These are often only one sentence long.

3 a) Do you think there is any bias in the article? Is the journalist totally neutral, or can you detect her point of view?

   b) How might a writer's point of view come across without that view being openly expressed?
   Look at:
- the choice of headline
- the amount of space devoted to each point of view
- how the article ends.

Serious practice

Practise using the four-paragraph structure in the unit activity.

UNIT ACTIVITY 3.7 Write a report for your local council on a plan to pedestrianise your local shopping centre (i.e. ban all cars from a pedestrian area). Your report represents the views of local youth groups.

USEFUL WORDS AND PHRASES

Some important opposites are used in this unit. Learn the pairs of words listed below. They will will be useful when you analyse texts and write your own pieces.

Words to describe the tone (the attitude of the writer)

Personal	*Impersonal*
Subjective	*Objective*
Emotionally involved	*Detached*
Passionate	*Dispassionate*
Biased	*Neutral, unbiased, balanced*

Words to describe the style (the way language is used)

Informal, colloquial	*Formal*
First person (I, we)	*Third person* (he, she, it, they)
Active verbs	*Passive verbs*

For example, *The dog bit the man* (active), *The man was bitten by the dog* (passive)

The words on the left-hand side might well describe an argumentative or persuasive piece of writing, where the writer is committed to a point of view. The words on the right-hand side describe analytical writing.

Hints

- Read the question carefully. Identify the words which refer to the purpose, the audience and the form of the writing.
- As the report writer, you should remain neutral and present the arguments for and against in a balanced way.
- You can, of course, report the views of others, either directly by quoting their actual words in speech marks, or indirectly by summarising their views (*Local traders said that . . .*).
- Your conclusion may contain a recommendation following a consideration of all the evidence.

Unit 3.8
Effective openings

The unit activity is to write a character profile with particular attention to an arresting opening (see page 133).

(see page 133)

Extract
A

Here there are mostly facts, but can you identify where opinions creep in? Does the review writer assume that the readers have specialist knowledge of the subject? In which publications might you find this type of writing?

Having reformed as a group after success with *Charge* and *That's Enough*, Rik Salt and Dave Pepper have employed producer Will Stutters to mix their debut album. The result is sunny funk samples and out-there beat technology hung over loose-limbed rap songs about being young.

Extract
B

This example starts with a rhetorical question, and this sets the tone for a quite hostile review.

Why do the Fruitcake sisters always sing about themselves? This album consists of endless tributes to sisterly love and snapshots of life in trendy Islington. It's like a North London edition of *Hello!* magazine. The girls have gone for string'n'synth soaked emo-pop stoked with skipping beats and glossy choruses.

Making a start

The opening of a piece of writing should set the tone for the whole piece. We will look at reviews as an example.

Reviews

Here are the opening lines from some reviews of television shows, films and CDs. Can you tell immediately whether the review will be complimentary in tone, or critical?

1   *It is not often that I use the word 'genius' about a young director's first film.*
2   *I suppose there is a market out there for bland, middle of the road music which soothes rather than excites.*
3   *This is the third solo album since the group split.*
4   *This is a dreadful film.*
5   *It's always sad to see a once great performer taking on one tour too many.*

Activity 3.8a   Link the following types of opening with the examples above.

a) Factual
b) Descriptive
c) Hard-hitting statement of opinion
d) Sarcastic, sneering
e) Admiring
f) Half-hearted, mixed opinions
g) Use of strong adjectives
h) Sad and regretful

Get it off your chest, or keep them in suspense?

If you write a review you are going to pass judgement on someone else's work. There are two ways you could approach a review:

- express your view strongly in the opening sentence or two, then support that view with example and detail
- start with fact and descriptive detail, putting the subject into context, and arrive at a judgement later.

For example, look at Extracts A and B opposite.

Activity 3.8b   1   Think of a piece of music, a film, a book or a television programme, and write the opening paragraph for a review targeted at your age group. It is best to choose a topic about which you have strong feelings. Write up to four sentences.
2   Experiment with different types of opening, using ideas from the extracts above.

Another type of review involves reconsidering a course of action or a procedure. For an example, look at the following question:

> Your school has a rule governing movement around the school in busy corridors. It states that students should keep to the left and observe a one-way system on staircases. However, the rule is not working in practice.
>
> Write a report for senior managers of the school reviewing this rule, arriving at some points for change

Here are some possible openings for this report. Each one has its merits.

A   *Look, it's no good pretending. The rule just doesn't work. Here's why.*
B   *It has become clear for some time that the rule governing movement around the school is not working.*
C   *Will it take a serious injury to a younger student before the senior management gets off its backside and takes notice?*
D   *We are concerned that there will be a serious injury to a student if the school rule regarding movement in corridors is not amended.*
E   *We hope the senior management will not be offended if we point out that they are rarely seen at the top of the main stairwell when the bell goes at 11.20 on a Tuesday.*

Activity 3.8c

1   With a partner, decide which opening would be most effective for the answer to the question.
2   Think of a school or college rule which you think needs changing. Write a report for the senior management analysing the rule and suggesting amendments to it.
    Experiment with different styles of opening. Then write four or five paragraphs.

What makes someone tick?

One interesting area of writing to analyse, review and comment is the character profile. Newspapers often have a 'Comment and Analysis' page which might contain articles about people in the news. These articles try to get beyond biographical facts to provide a profile of a personality.

Personality profiles analyse the facts about a person's life, and include comment on their's personality and behaviour.

Serious practice

UNIT ACTIVITY 3.8   Write a character profile of someone whom you know and admire.

Planning your writing

Gathering ideas

Your aim is to get beyond the biographical facts (date of birth, etc.) to reveal the personality beneath the surface. The sort of questions you might address are:

• How have background and education shaped the subject's personality? Who, for example, does the person consider to be the greatest influences on him/her?
• What are the person's values and/or beliefs?
• What ambitions does the person have?
• What do friends and colleagues think about this person?

Paragraph plan

A straightforward plan for your writing might be:

- **Paragraph 1**
  Identify the subject, saying why this person interests you.
- **Paragraph 2**
  Biographical details
- **Paragraph 3**
  Qualities you admire, using examples of the person's behaviour to illustrate these qualities, for example:

  Even though it would have been easier for my grandad to have shut down the business and returned to his parents, he persevered and eventually made a success of it. This shows his determination, courage and self-belief.

- **Paragraph 4**
  A summary of the person's chief qualities.

THE OPENING

You want to interest your readers immediately in your subject, so you need to find an effective way of grabbing their attention. Consider using one of these possible openings:

- You could start with an anecdote, a story which illustrates typical behaviour of your subject, for example:

  You will have seen this person loping down the corridors. He seems to know everyone, from the smallest, most timid eleven year old to the teacher about to retire after thirty years at the school.

- You could involve the reader personally by addressing the reader directly, for example:

  Picture the scene: a hot Friday afternoon with forty minutes to go before the bell. There is a mood of boredom and anticipation. Suddenly a familiar cry erupts from the other end of the lab, followed by a bang and a cloud of smoke. He has struck again.

- You could start with a sad, nostalgic mood, as if the person is now gone, for example:

  I remember her smile mostly. It made everyone feel warm. It is still the first thing I think of whenever someone mentions her name.

- You could give straightforward factual detail, for example:

  My uncle was born in 1953 in Glamorgan, South Wales. He left school at fifteen and became a miner.

- You could start with a quotation, and introduce some suspense and surprise to intrigue the reader, for example:

  'Obstinate and pig-headed' was how this person was first described to me. That was before I had met her, and I soon found out why people said that.

Choose one of these techniques, or devise one of your own. Remember that the opening you choose will largely determine the success of the whole piece of writing.

WHAT EXAMINERS ARE LOOKING FOR

In judging the overall effectiveness of a piece of writing, examiners look at the opening to see how the topic is introduced to the reader.

Unit 3.9
Developing your writing

The unit activity is to write an analytical article (see page 137).

Extract **A**

This is the opening of the article.

Growing up on the front line

Vincent Stott, at 17 the youngest British soldier in the Gulf, has come home. What is his legacy of war? Joan Simpson reports.

Fear, a 17-year-old soldier reflects, is 'something I have looked at, and nothing much will ever worry me again'. Private Vincent Stott is home from the war. Vivid in his memory, in the place where teenage lads on civvy street might relish a match-winning goal or a cricket triumph, is the din of battle and the images of destruction and death on the front line of the Gulf war.

Pte Stott is a reluctant witness in recalling the events which have hastened his maturity. He shrugs off the fame that was thrust upon him by dint of his being the youngest British soldier at the front line in the Gulf. 'It's just my job. I'm only doing what I'm trained for.'

Extract **B**

Having interested the reader in a specific individual, the journalist then turns to the issue: should 17-year-olds be risked on the front line? She gives the argument against, then in the next paragraph gives Private Stott's response to that argument.

The argument ran that, because soldiers under the age of 18 are not allowed to serve in Northern Ireland, they should not be sent to a war by politicians whom they are not old enough to vote in or out of office. The age limit for Ireland is deemed necessary because of the more complicated decisions which may face young soldiers as they patrol the streets.

Pte Stott stonily dismisses the arguments of those who thought to shield him from the desert war. His father, Tom, a former member of the Royal Scots in which his son now serves, proudly backs him up. 'Should I worry more about my son when he is 17 than when he is 18?'

Extract **C**

This section reports the view of the young soldiers' commanding officer.

Lieutenant-colonel Iain Johnstone says: 'They grew to such stature and reached such dizzy heights. As far as I am concerned if they are good enough to be a Royal Scot they were good enough to go to the Gulf. None of them acted like little boys, they had done all their training, they were fit, motivated and very professional. Their age did not worry me in the slightest.'

Extract D

The next section of the report returns to the experiences of Private Stott and his colleagues. There are anecdotes to bring the events to life.

They took prisoners as they went and it is ironic that what shocked them was that 'some enemy troops were really quite old – three of the ones we took were over 50, they were ragged and had only some crusts of bread. But you could not feel sorry for them, they were still the enemy.'

Extract E

The final section sums up the effect of such experiences on the young soldiers.

Pte Morris has not yet got around to seeing his old school friends, years behind him now in experience of life. Pte Quate has been out for a drink with his old school pals but felt 'older than them and I didn't like to talk too much about what I had done'.

Pte Stott, too, has stuck with army friends. His father says he has changed, become more grown up and more cynical. Pte Stott gives a rare, brilliant grin of agreement.

In what way does he feel he has changed? 'I have faced the war, learnt as a soldier. Yes, I have learnt to control fear'.

from The Times, *10 April 1991*

BACKGROUND INFORMATION
The article is from the time of the 1991 Gulf War. There was at that time a debate in the press about whether soldiers as young as 17 should be in the front line of battle. The article analyses the issue by focusing firstly on the experiences of one 17-year-old soldier. Some people were outraged that 17-year-olds were exposed to the horrors of warfare; others thought that the young soldiers matured quickly because of their experiences and showed no ill-effects.

Making a start

In Unit 1.9 and other units, you have seen how signpost words and phrases can be used to link ideas so that your writing develops logically. This unit looks at the development of ideas in one article. It has been split into five extracts so you can identify clearly how it develops.

Activity 3.9a

1 From the tone of the opening paragraphs in Extract A, do you think the journalist is neutral, or does she take sides in the debate?
2 How does the journalist quickly establish Private Stott as a modest, courageous young man, rather embarrassed at the attention he has received?

Look at how the rather old-fashioned vocabulary and phrases give the soldier a mythical, heroic image: 'teenage lads', 'civvy street', 'the din of battle', 'hastened his maturity', 'by dint of his being', 'shrugs off the fame'.

Other techniques used to establish the tone of the report include:

- quotations from Private Stott
- an arresting first word
- the use of contrast between his life as a soldier and a typical 17-year-old's life
- the use of emotional statements which seem to link him with great heroic events from the past: 'Private Vincent Stott is home from the war.'

In some respects this report is typical of the sort of analytical writing you might be asked to write: an assignment to consider both sides of an issue, perhaps in the form of a newspaper article. Like the journalist, you, too, would need to plan how to develop your writing into an effective exploration of the topic.

Activity 3.9b

1 Look for these features in the report:

a) a main *headline* and a *sub-headline*. Are the headlines neutral, or do they give any clue to the writer's own views?

b) *stories of individuals.* The writer hangs the report on these rather than just giving abstract arguments. Do you think that this makes the report more interesting? Why?

c) *short interviews to present views.* She reports other people's views, not her own.

2 Look at how the report develops:

a) *Interest the reader in an individual.* We are not only given facts, we also become emotionally involved in Pte Stott's life (see Activity 3.9a).

b) *Introduce the issue* – in this case, should 17-year-olds be allowed to fight and possibly die for their country?

c) *Both sides of the argument are presented* – but which side is given more space and explanation?

d) *Come back to Pte Stott,* with more of his and others' experiences. Bring their stories to life by presenting them in their own words, in speech marks.

e) Finally, *get individuals to reflect* on what they have learnt from their experiences.

f) *Look for a neat ending.* In this case, the report ends with the words of Pte Stott – but what do you notice about the very last word?

These techniques of developing ideas – and giving the piece a satisfying structure – could be applied to many types of analytical or commentary writing.

Activity 3.9c

Is this really a balanced, impartial piece of analytical writing? How far do the writer's views actually come through?

Discuss with your group: What do you think Joan Simpson's views are about whether 17-year-olds should be fighting in the front line? Look for evidence in the report to support your views.

Serious practice

Here is an activity to give you practice in the techniques described in this unit. The topic is related to the one in the report, but it is given a twist.

UNIT ACTIVITY 3.9 'Should women be allowed to fight in the front line, whether in the army, navy or air force?'

Write an analytical article presenting the pros and cons of this topic.

Hints

- Read the question carefully. Identify the words which refer to the purpose, the audience and the form of the writing.
- You are not arguing for or against this statement, although you do need a grasp of the issues to do the activity properly.

- It would be a good idea to have a class or group discussion, generating ideas by arguing a particular point of view.
- To stimulate some ideas, read Extract F. It is a letter from a reader of the newspaper where you work. You could refer to it, or interview the writer, in your report.

Extract
F

Do not put women in war zones

As a sub-lieutenant in the Second World War, I would like to say from experience that women should not serve at sea in wartime. They have much to contribute in support roles, but at sea they could be a liability.

How would a male sailor react to seeing a woman comrade's blood splattered on the deck during action with the enemy?

My first ship was torpedoed in 1941. For ten hours we were under murderous air attack and shelling from shore. I have seen my comrades' blood and guts flowing in the scuppers. I would have been demoralised if that had been a female crew member.

It is unrealistic to expect female crew members to carry large, heavy shells and pieces of equipment. They are simply not made for that.

To send women sailors to sea on warships is a triumph of political correctness over common sense.

Yours faithfully

WRITING YOUR ARTICLE

- Use ideas and techniques from the report on young soldiers. You could use it as a model when considering how to develop your own writing.
- Remember to start with a headline and sub-headline.
- Remember not to state your views – you are presenting the views of others and exploring the implications.
- Look back to earlier units for advice on linking your ideas, especially pages 16, 41, 93 and 104, where signpost words and phrases are listed.
- You will probably want to include some interviews with, or short quotations from, imaginary people. Look back to the report by Joan Simpson for tips on setting out.

  Do not use a question-and-answer format. Try to integrate the quotations into the rest of the article. For example, look at the first sentence of Extract A – the quotation from Pte Stott flows without a break from the first half of the sentence. In other places, the quotation comes first, followed by a simple phrase such as *Private Stott says*. Note that *says* is in the present tense.

WHAT EXAMINERS ARE LOOKING FOR

Do you use the full range of punctuation available? In GCSE mark schemes, 'control of punctuation is secure, with some variety' describes grade C, while 'control of punctuation is effective, with a variety of marks used to enhance communication' describes grade A.

Unit 3.10
Writing technique: language and layout

The unit activity is to write a review (see page 141).

(see page 141).

Extract A

'Da Ali G Show' gets crazy

YO, YO, YO!

Ali G is wigged out and wonderful. He's one insane-in-the-brain hip-hop prankster supreme. If you're not laughin', I'm lyin'. And you'll be laughin' out loud with this wickedly rowdy clown.

He'll put a dizzy chucklehead spell on you.

(Deep breath. Continue raving)

'Da Ali G Show' starts rocking the late-night comedy house at 12.30 tonight on HBO. The show's wizard is British comic Sacha Baron Cohen, who has already created a giggly sensation in England.

Cohen's infamous alter ego, Ali G, is a self-styled 'hip-hop journalist' who sports a garish yellow track suit, wraparound glasses, a pullover hat and a bagful of slangy, surreal patter.

Somehow, some way, Cohen and his raucous Ali G persona manage to land interviews with real-life celebrities. Most of the famous folks interviewed appear somewhat clueless as they're being conned, though Boutrous Boutrous Ghali knows something odd is happening when Ali G asks, 'Is Disneyland a member of the United Nations?'

Is all of this sometimes politically incorrect in the hilarious extreme? Absolutely. With 'Da Ali G Show' HBO give Cohen an opportunity to crisscross America for a screwball U.S. edition of the hit UK series. It's inventive, unpredictable and loonily shameless.

Say howdy to what may be the funniest British comedy invasion since Monty Python.

from Detroit Free Press, *1 February 2003: www.freep.com*

Extract B

Go home 'Da Ali G Show'

British comedian invades U.S. television with annoying satire

First, in the interest of international relations, an obvious truth must be acknowledged: Britain has a glorious tradition of satire.

Jonathan Swift alone would place the kingdom in the lampooners' hall of fame. Flash forward to Monty Python, Eddie Izzard and *Absolutely Fabulous* and our admiration is boundless.

Which brings us, regretfully, to 'Da Ali G Show'. Nice to meet you, Mr Cohen. Now go home. Please.

At first, we admit, we got a kick out of the characters you've created: hip-hop journalist Ali G, resplendent in acid-yellow track suit and big jewellery; clueless Borat of Kazakhstan.

But when Cohen goes in search of America, 'Da Ali G Show' goes terribly wrong. Yes, this dumb and dumber style of humour is now available in an imported version and HBO (those chumps!) shelled out money for it.

The annoying aspect is that Cohen is talented and obviously capable of mining more than cheap laughs. But if he's already a hit, why should he work harder than audiences ask, at home or abroad?

For the HBO series, Cohen used his anonymity in America to snare interviews with prominent figures. Then he proceeds to squander the opportunities.

Those hoodwinked by 'Da Ali G Show' can shrug off the experience. But consider the larger insult and injury.

Ian Nathan in *The Times* last year wrote, 'Satire now concerns itself with daft teenage role-play and pushing the boundaries of taste'.

Nothing funny about that. Much like 'Da Ali G Show'.

adapted from The Cincinnati Enquirer, 21 February 2003: www.enquirer.com

Making a start

So you have planned your essay, thought of an effective opening, and have some idea of how the writing will develop. To convince your reader, you also need some techniques of language.

Extracts A and B are two reviews of the same television programme. They differ not only in their opinions of the show, but also in the language they use. Both are written in distinctive styles. They are American, and have a different tone to the types of review you will find in most British publications.

SATIRE

Extract B uses the word *satire*. But what is it?

A satire is a piece of writing or a dramatic production which criticises people's behaviour or attitudes by holding them up to scorn or ridicule. *Lampoon* is another word for a satire.

Jonathan Swift wrote one of the most famous satirical books, *Gulliver's Travels*, in which he criticised England by disguising it as Lilliput, a country inhabited by midgets who behave absurdly and cruelly.

Activity 3.10a

1   Look again at Extract A. It is clearly not written in Standard English! Copy the table and find examples of the following features of language and tone:

Feature	Example
The writing imitates speech	
Use of slang expressions	
Lots of adjectives, sometimes in lists	
Exploits the sounds of words using techniques such as: • alliteration • occasional rhyme	
Positive and enthusiastic tone; no negative comments	
Confident, exaggerated expression of views	

2   Look at Extract B. This review has a more formal tone. Copy the table and find examples of the following features of language and tone:

Feature	Example
Use of the first person plural *we*	
Pained, regretful tone	
Sometimes written as if speaking to Sacha Baron Cohen	
Some positive comments	
Outweighed by negative comments	
Places programme in tradition of earlier imported British programmes. Makes comparisons.	

Mixed reviews

Reviewers will often disagree on the merits of their subject, especially when comedy is involved. Reviewer B *dislikes* 'Da Ali G Show' because it is shameless, with no boundaries of good taste; reviewer A *likes* the show for those very same reasons!

Reviewing is obviously a personal matter. Most readers prefer a balanced approach and a calm tone, to a ranting, over-hostile or over-favourable review. A reviewer will often point out good qualities, even if the overall impact of the subject under review is disappointing.

If you look in any newspaper, you will find a surprising amount of writing to review. Here is a list of the subjects of review in one daily newspaper:

- films
- television programmes
- books
- radio programmes
- restaurants and bars
- plays
- holiday companies
- live concerts
- ballet
- opera
- CDs
- art exhibitions
- cars and motorbikes
- comedy acts
- clubs.

There are a lot of judgements being made by reviewers!

Serious practice

Now here is your opportunity to be the reviewer and to use the language features highlighted in this unit.

UNIT ACTIVITY 3.10   Choose a topic from the list on page 140 and write a review.

 LANGUAGE TECHNIQUES
Here are extracts from critics' reviews to illustrate some of the language techniques you could use in your review.

> 'After last year's debacle of supposed trailblazers Fischerspooner, electro-clash returned with a vengeance and became everything it was supposed to be — sleazy, retro-future dance music.'
>
> (Metro, 21 February 2003)

Note the structure of this opening sentence: long build-up, leading to snappy judgement.

> 'Although the piece threatens to lose its way, this is terrific fringe theatre, beautifully inventive and very, very funny.'
>
> (Metro, 21 February 2003)

'Although' introduces a slightly critical note, but this leads to a positive, enthusiastic overall judgement.

> 'As practical as it is, with that motor, that suspension, and that look, the Dragster was built for the style-conscious with a dark side.'

An effective final sentence which uses a list to summarise the qualities of the motorbike.

> 'So why do I find this restaurant so spiritless? Because it's all looking a bit same old, same old, that's why. This offering, brought to us by the people behind Cinnamon City, is so formulaic it could have been dreamed up by a drone of marketing men.'
>
> (Metro, 25 February 2003)

Notice the use of a question to set up the answer and the use of repetition for effect.

WHAT EXAMINERS ARE LOOKING FOR

The chosen publication for your review will help you decide on the style you should adopt. Examiners look for this adaptability. Here is one of the descriptions of grade A writing: 'The register is fully appropriate to the needs of the audience and the writing is assured in its style'.

Register means the type of language you use in certain situations. How formal do you need to be? What level of knowledge and understanding do you expect your readers or listeners to have?

Hints

- Think about the purpose, audience and form of your writing.
- You should specify a publication where this review would appear. This would help you decide on the technical or specialised knowledge you expect of your readers.
- The topic could be school-based, such as a mock restaurant critic's account of school lunches, or a review of a school production.
- The judgement you make should be fair. This means that it might be hostile, but it should not involve a personal attack. It can be respectful as well as critical.

Unit 3.11
Effective endings

The unit activity is to write a commentary (see page 145).

 Extract A It seems that excessive television viewing can make a child apathetic and passive, but it is equally true that children learn a lot from television. This is not just from serious documentaries but from the soaps as well: about relationships, families, emotions. So is it a matter of parents not banning their children from watching television, but of talking to them about their viewing so that family relationships are strengthened?

 Extract B Certainly the rise in violent crime is disturbing, and many people think it is linked to children's viewing habits. This can of course never be proven, but you do have to wonder whether watching ten violent fictional scenes a night – plus seeing some real violence on the news – does not give a child a disturbing message about how to tackle problems.

 Extract C Despite watching all that violence and drama, children are still sensitive about friendships, family relationships and the death of pets. Television has not apparently made children numb and unfeeling, and maybe adults are unnecessarily worried about its effects. Perhaps adults are rather hypocritical in their concern about what their watch. As one parent put it to me: 'Like most parents I worry about what my children are watching – but I'd be devastated if you tried to take my telly away.'

Making a start

Coming up with an effective ending is one of the most difficult of all writing skills. Many students repeat the opening, or simply stop. Such an unsatisfactory ending leaves the reader with a poor impression of the whole piece of writing.

Look back to Unit 3.9, which includes an article entitled 'Growing up on the front line'. Do you remember that it began and ended with the same word – *fear*? That was a neat way of highlighting one of the main themes of the report, but such inspiration does not always come to you at the right time, especially not during GCSE English examinations! What you need is a few ideas for endings which you can adapt to any given writing assignment.

An effective ending will do one or more of the following:

1   It could summarise the main points or ideas of the essay.
2   It may restate the main idea in a different way.
3   It will be in keeping with the form of writing (for example, a speech or a letter).
4   It could challenge or involve the reader.
5   It might balance the pros and cons of the issue neatly, especially if this happens to be an analytical piece.
6   It could pose a question.
7   It could be in the form of a quotation in speech marks.
8   It could be a warning.

It is better to consider an effective ending as not just the last sentence, but as being the whole final paragraph, perhaps around three to four sentences in length. This allows you to build up a final impression to leave with your reader.

Imagine this analytical assignment:

Consider the effects of television on young people. Write an article for a school magazine analysing the possible benefits and harmful effects which could arise from a solid diet of television.

Activity 3.11a   Extracts A–C on the facing page show possible final paragraphs using the techniques listed above.

1   a)   With a partner, decide which of the techniques listed above are used in these three final paragraphs.
    b)   From those short paragraphs alone, which do you think makes the most effective ending?
    c)   Which technique used here are you most likely to use in your next essay to round-off the writing?
2   Look back to earlier units in this section. Choose one of the unit activities which you have written to analyse, review and comment. Rewrite the ending using one or more of the techniques listed above.

Serious practice

UNIT ACTIVITY 3.11   Write an essay commenting on how the rise in use of mobile phones has affected our lives.

Hints

◆   A brainstorm or mind map will help you to generate and link ideas on this topic. Use the ideas in *Planning your writing* (page 144) to get you started.

◆   Pay special attention to the final paragraph. See *Paragraph plan* (page 145).
◆   Read Extract D (page 144).

Extract D

Saved from 9,000 miles away

Darren Alcock was travelling alone in Western Australia. He set off on a three-hour walk to the summit of Bluff Knoll. After 25 minutes he reached the summit, and drizzle and fog set in. For an hour and a half he wandered aimlessly.

Eventually he called his dad 9,000 miles away in England. His dad told him to phone the local emergency services, but Darren didn't because he felt rather silly. Luckily his father did call the local police in Australia. They called Darren, but his phone went dead within five seconds with a flat battery. Darren's father had told the police where he was, and the district emergency rescue team was sent to find him. It was by then dark, cold and raining. Darren sheltered under an overhanging rock, shone his torch in the air and shouted. On the point of giving up their search, they found him. The local mobile-phone mast had only been put up the week before.

Planning your writing

Gathering ideas

Here are some ideas on mobile phones:

- They are useful for personal safety.
- You could imagine situations where a mobile phone can save people's lives. There is a debate amongst mountaineers, explorers and those who venture into the wilderness as to whether it is ethical to take mobile phones into such places. Does it take away the element of risk which is supposed to be part of the appeal of dangerous pursuits? Or is it simply a sensible precaution?
- They are convenient for social arrangements.
- They speed up business arrangements and help the local and national economy.
- They have given us greater mobility by avoiding delays and misunderstandings.
- They have become fashion accessories, not just boring telephones.
- Some people find them a nuisance and an irritant, for example in the theatre, cinema, restaurants, trains, schools.
- Text messaging has led to the development of a new type of language.
- Text messages are cheap and instant.
- Overall they have changed our attitudes towards communication.

In discussion groups you will be able to come up with more ideas which can be added to your mind map.

Paragraph plan

Once you have collected the ideas and decided which you want to include, you should think about how to arrange them into four or five paragraphs, each with a topic sentence. Avoid simply listing the ideas. Try to include an example from your or others' experience to support each separate point you make, for example:

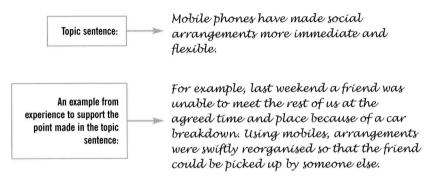

Topic sentence: → *Mobile phones have made social arrangements more immediate and flexible.*

An example from experience to support the point made in the topic sentence: → *For example, last weekend a friend was unable to meet the rest of us at the agreed time and place because of a car breakdown. Using mobiles, arrangements were swiftly reorganised so that the friend could be picked up by someone else.*

This essay comes under the category of *comment*. This means that you do not have to present a neutral, balanced account, but can include your own views as you progress. However, you will want to consider both sides of the topic.

Your *final paragraph* should summarise the main points you have made, and also make a general judgement about whether the mobile phone is a social trend with more benefits than ill-effects. You might also look to the future and consider how technology will develop: video facility on mobile phones, for example.

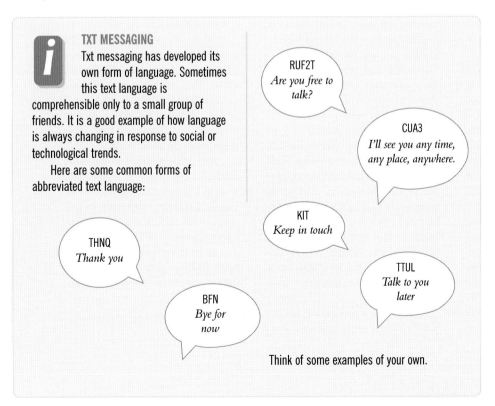

TXT MESSAGING

Txt messaging has developed its own form of language. Sometimes this text language is comprehensible only to a small group of friends. It is a good example of how language is always changing in response to social or technological trends.

Here are some common forms of abbreviated text language:

RUF2T
Are you free to talk?

CUA3
I'll see you any time, any place, anywhere.

KIT
Keep in touch

THNQ
Thank you

TTUL
Talk to you later

BFN
Bye for now

Think of some examples of your own.

Unit 3.12

Bringing it all together

The unit activity is to write an essay to comment (see page 149).

Despite schools' efforts to integrate pupils from different racial, economic and social backgrounds, inner-city teenagers are still dividing themselves into tribes.
Caroline Haydon *reports*

D'ya wanna be in my gang?

It was the pale-blue collar with pointed metal spikes that did it. Until then I had tried to accommodate my daughter's attempts to keep up with the local gang. But now she wanted to lead the gang. And she had a chosen style – to me it seemed sub-punk – dog collars, spikes, 'hoodies' proclaiming band names, baggy jeans and coloured hair. They called themselves grungers – not a term I recognised.

But my daughter was only twelve. And her father and I drew the line at the pale-blue collar she'd bought at London's Camden Lock market, suggesting she might catch her chin on the spikes.

Recognise the description? The chances are that if you are a parent in the London area or any major town, you will. Grungers and their avowed enemies, the townies or trendies (who favour different music and designer sports gear) have invaded our schools and imported into the classroom the fashions and idioms of the street – and some of its roudier elements, too.

For those with children starting secondary school, it can be alarming. I wasn't the only parent to be taken aback by the extreme fashions and by the virulence of feeling between the groups. The children themselves can be shocked by the intensity of it all. And parents might mind very much which

tribe their pre-teen or teenager chooses. As my daughter put it: 'What tribe you are shows in how you dress, your attitudes towards life and school – whether you are disruptive or not – your accent and how you perform. If you're a townie it's often cool not to do work or be sent out of class, so they can be disruptive in lessons.'

But parents beware – all experiences are not the same. The tribe that is disruptive in one school might be on the side of the angels in another. One mother told of her daughter's rocky introduction to gang life at her school. Ellie had fallen foul of a sub-group of grungers called Goths, who wear black. 'When she was younger it made her quite miserable,' she says. 'She had to be in her tribe – the trendies – to be safe.'

For the comprehensive schools, with their wider social intake, it doesn't look as if the gangs are good news. Just when you thought a comprehensive could succeed at integrating pupils from every race or class background, along comes a social trend that positively obstructs that aim.

'There are go-betweens and outsiders, but if you're a go-between you may not be popular,' says my daughter. 'If you want to be noticed you have to be in one group or another.'

So is any of this new? The clinical psychologist Oliver James is pretty convinced that this is all a continuation of a very old story.

'Where any teenagers are gathered there will be subgroups. At that age you are trying to define yourself over and above what your parents or class dictates, trying to define your identity," he says. "Paradoxically, in your attempt to be an individual you find your identity through other groups.'

And girls experience all this more intensely. 'Appearance is a matter of great importance to all teenagers but, despite feminism, girls still gain a considerable amount of self- and peer-esteem through appearance.'

So far, so run-of-the-mill, then. It's tough being a parent. But if you're worried, take heart. It is only a phase.

adapted from The Independent, *31 October 2002*

Extract B

I live in West London, I'm 13 years old and I'm in Year 9. I was amazed how aware a journalist was about the crowds found in schools.

I have several comments. First, Townies are sometimes known as Gazzas and Shazzas, which comes from the names Gary and Sharon, and are more commonly known as the Shazzas. This is because the two names are common in Townies' families; Grungers are sometimes known as Charlies for the same reason.

Second, most year 11s are still faithful to their crowd, and take it as seriously as younger pupils. Third, you didn't mention Trushoes, one of the most common crowds. These consist of people who are

Grungers vs Townies

sometimes extremely popular, but dress as normally as possible. I suppose they are what you might call Go-betweeners, but they are not nerds.

Fourth, you seem to be suggesting that you need to be in a crowd if you want to be accepted and not hassled. Well, neither I nor my friends are in any crowd. We have our individual style. We may not be popular but that is not hard to deal with.

Finally, I think Townies become Townies because that is what their parents were. Ditto Grungers. I think it is all quite pathetic. I believe that teachers should be more in touch with these issues.

Extract C

In my school there are not many Grungers. The school consists mostly of Townies and Skaters. I thought I'd tell you about me, a typical Grunger. I have been called many things including Greeb, Goth, Rocker and Mosha. The reason that I dress the way I do and think how I think, is because of

anger, stress, rage and frustration. I want to break free.

I use music as an escape. Without the music – grunge, heavy metal and rock – I would be nothing. I would still have all these painful feelings inside ….

Extract D

I am 16 years old and I agreed with Caroline Haydon's article, except for one thing. She suggested that school tribes existed only in 'London … or any major town'. Well, I live close to Cheddar, a medium-sized village in Somerset, and you can be sure as eggs are eggs that if you went into Cheddar on a school day you would come across a wide variety of groups: Townies, Skaters, Grungers (as you called them), Jocks, Goths and a few other small, separate groups.

There are also a large number of 'normal', casual people who dress in casual clothes, which includes me. The Go-betweens are not the unpopular ones in my school – the Townies and Goths are. The popular ones are the Skaters and the 'normal' kids, so, unlike what your article said, to be 'noticed' we don't actually have to be full-on Goths, Townies or members of any other large 'tribe'.

ANALYSIS OR COMMENT?
Remind yourself of the difference between these two types of writing. Which sections of Extract B would you say fall into the *analyse* category, and which into *comment*?

- Read the question you choose carefully. Identify the words which tell you about the purpose, audience and form of the writing.
- Consider the ideas suggested in *Gathering ideas* below.
- Consider the suggested plans in *Paragraph plan*, below.

Making a start

Read Extracts A–D, which are about gangs and social groups in schools. These form the source material for the unit activity, where you can practise the skills you have learnt in Units 3.1–3.11.

Extract A analyses a social trend, but not in a detached, impersonal way. The writer's daughter is involved, so she is also in the role of concerned parent. There is therefore a lot of comment as well. The language is not the formal language of an analytical report, and some of the words chosen give away a point of view. For example, what impression is given by the word *invaded* in the third paragraph?

Extracts B, C and D are letters, also from *The Independent*, written in response to the article in Extract A.

Serious practice

UNIT ACTIVITY 3.12 Choose **one** of these tasks.

1 Comment on the 'tribes' in your school. Draw on the information and views in the pieces of writing above, and your own experience.
2 Analyse the appeal of belonging to 'tribes' such as those described.

Once you have chosen a task, decide whether you wish to write a speech for a school debating competition or a letter to *The Independent*.

Planning your writing

Gathering ideas

Here is some research material you could include:

- You may be able to refer to your reading in other areas of the GCSE English or English Literature course. For example *Lord of the Flies* has much to say about the appeal of tribes, and about how the tribe can affect an individual's behaviour. *Romeo and Juliet* also has tribal rivalry as its social and cultural setting.
- You could carry out some research into gangs and tribes from earlier eras. For example, the Teddy Boys of the 1950s, the Mods and Rockers of the 1960s and 1970s. Interviews with people who remember those times would add interest to your writing.

Paragraph plan

Consider these paragraph plans:

For Question 1:

- **Paragraph 1: Introduction**
  Introduction for the general reader who knows little about the topic, such as your teacher.
- **Paragraphs 2–4**
  Describe the characteristics of appearance, speech and behaviour of the main groups (two or three paragraphs).
- **Paragraph 5: Conclusion**
  Comment on the influence – positive or negative – of such groups on the school as a whole and on the lives of individuals.

For Question 2:

- **Paragraph 1: Introduction**
  Introduce the topic.
- **Paragraph 2**
  Use information from the pieces in this unit – and your own experience – to describe the types of groups found in schools. For each, you should explain the 'appeal' for a certain type of person.
- **Paragraph 3**
  A more general paragraph analysing the pros and cons of groups.
- **Paragraph 4: Conclusion**
  Your conclusion could pull together the areas you have explored by listing the main factors that appeal to people about belonging to a 'tribe'.

 BEFORE YOU START WRITING …
Remind yourself about you have learnt in earlier units, in particular:

- Unit 3.5, choosing an appropriate style
- Unit 3.7, planning your writing
- Unit 3.8, how to write an effective opening, and Unit 3.11, an effective ending

- Unit 3.9, developing your ideas in your writing
- Unit 3.10, language techniques to make your writing varied and convincing.

WHAT EXAMINERS ARE LOOKING FOR
In all tasks, examiners will look for a 'clear focus on relevant points', such as examples of advantages and disadvantages of belonging to distinctive groups.

Glossary

abstract noun
A word which names feelings or ideas, for example: *love*, *hatred*, *liberty*

anecdote
A true story from personal experience

antithesis
The balancing of words or ideas with opposite meanings, for example, good/evil; joy/sadness

argument
A reason or series of reasons used to support an opinion or a proposition

assertion
Bold statement of something which might be contentious

audience
Those for whom a piece of writing or a speech is intended

colloquial
A style of writing which imitates everyday conversation; informal

debate
An argument which follows accepted rules: a proposer speaks in favour of a proposition; an opposer speaks against; each is supported by a seconder. A chairperson oversees and keeps order

diction
The choice of words used; vocabulary

emotional
Governed by feelings rather than rational thought

emotive language
Language which produces an emotional response, for example *gang of thugs* rather than *group of people*

fact
A truth; a real state of things; a statement which can be checked for its truth

form of writing
A specific type of writing with its own conventions of layout and style, for example, letter, leaflet, article

imagery
The use of simile, metaphor and/or personification to make writing vivid

imperative
The form of a verb used for commands, requests or advice, such as *Pass the salt*, *Sit up!*, *Visit the Bishop's Palace*. The imperative verb is usually the first word in the sentence.

linguistic features
The features of language in writing, including puns, rhetorical questions, lists, irony, satire, rhythm, rhyme, allusion, emotive language

logical
Using sound reasoning to argue a point; opposite *illogical*

opinion
A belief, or view, with which other people may well disagree

oppose
To argue against a proposition

paragraph
Normally a collection of sentences linked by one idea or topic

parody
The copying of a writer's style

person
First person: *I*, *we*; second person: *you*; third person: *he*, *she*, *it*, *they*

propose
To argue in support of a proposition

proposition
A statement of opinion which is the starting-point for an argument

rational
Using reason; opposite *irrational*

readership
See *audience*

salutation
The greeting at the beginning of a letter, for example, *Dear Mrs Smith*

satire
Writing which criticises people's behaviour or attitudes by holding them up to scorn or ridicule

signpost words and phrases
Adverbs or adverbial phrases which guide the reader through a piece of writing by providing links between ideas, for example, *however*; *therefore*; also known as discourse markers or discursive markers

slang
A non-standard English word or expression normally used in speech, or in writing which imitates speech

structural features
The layout of a piece of writing, including headings, subheadings, organisation of paragraphs, varied length of sentences and paragraphs, bullet lists, indentation, style and size of fonts

style
A distinctive manner of writing; the language choices made by the writer for effect. A style of writing might, for example, be very formal and grammatically correct, or informal and colloquial

syntax
Sentence construction; the arrangement of words in grammatical sentences

tense
The form of the verb which indicates the time of the action, for example, *I go* (present); *I went* (past); *I will go* (future)

tone
The writer's attitude towards a topic. The tone, for example, might be serious, sarcastic, comic, etc.

topic sentence
The sentence which states the main idea within a paragraph; generally the first sentence in a paragraph

voice
Who is speaking in the writing

writing to advise
Writing to recommend a course of action

writing to analyse
Writing which examines an issue or a proposal from all angles, normally balanced and detached in tone

writing to argue
Using reasoning and logic to persuade someone to a point of view

writing to comment
Writing which makes critical remarks or observations on an issue or proposal

writing to describe
Writing which gives a clear account of people, places, events, feelings, experiences

writing to explain
Writing to make something plain, using detail to show how things are connected

writing to inform
Writing which uses facts and information to explain something

writing to persuade
Writing which attempts to influence the reader to a point of view or a course of action, usually more emotional in tone and technique than writing to argue

writing to review
writing which takes a close, critical look at, for example, a performance, a decision, a course of action; different from analytical writing because it usually involves a judgement, an expression of opinion

Sources and acknowledgements

Unit 1.1: from 'The Argument Clinic' in *Monty Python's Flying Circus: Just the* Words, Volume 2 (Methuen Books, 1998), reprinted by permission of the publisher; **Unit 1.2**: 'Is this advert too sick' from *The Express* (21 January 2000); 'Heroin baby' advertisement, reproduced by permission of Barnardo's; **Unit 1.3**: from letters to *Guardian Education* feature; 'Burns and Scalds' by Dr R. McConnell from www.studenthealth.co.uk info@StudentHealth.co.uk; **Unit 1.4**: from *The Big Issue* website, reprinted by permission of The Big Issue Company and The Big Issue Foundation; **Unit 1.5**: from Mike Sturbs, *Young People Now: June 1993* anthology, edited by Tim Burke (National Youth Agency), reprinted by permission of the publisher; from President John F. Kennedy's inauguration speech (20 January 1961) on www.barteby.com; **Unit 1.6**: letter from *The Independent* (2 May 1996), reprinted by permission of the publisher; from a speech by Tony Blair (1999); 'The Other Side of the Wall' by Angela Neusttater from *Telegraph Magazine* (22 April 2000); **Unit 1.8**: from *Fathers' Race: A Book About Paternity* by Charles Jennings (Abacus Books, 2000); from 'The Day I Broke My Car Habit' by George Monbiot in *The Guardian* (15 September 1999); **Unit 1.10**: an appeal letter from *Save the Children*, reprinted by permission of The Save the Children Fund; from 'Starting College? Heard about meningitis? Get immunised' – a Health Education Authority leaflet, © Health Education Authority 1999; **Unit 1.11**: from *Animal Farm* by George Orwell (Penguin Books, 1989); from *To Kill a Mockingbird* by Harper Lee (Arrow Books, 1989); from *Lord of the Flies* by William Golding (Faber & Faber, 1997); **Unit 1.12**: from 'More Wealth Less Aid' by Heather Stewart from *The Guardian* (30 November 2002), © *The Guardian*, reprinted by permission of the publisher; from 'Why Some Chocolate is Simply More Divine' by Jerome Monahan from *The Guardian* (15 October 2002), © Jerome Monahan, reprinted by permission of the publisher; from VSO advertisement on website www.vso.org.uk (10 February 2003); **Unit 2.1**: 'Seat Belts', based on Health Evidence Bulletins Wales, Hertfordshire Accident Prevention Group, School Transport News Online; **Unit 2.3**: from *The Whispering Land* by Gerald Durrell (Penguin Books, 1961); **Unit 2.4**: from *Scotts of Stow* catalogue (2003); from *The Independent Review* (26 December 2002), reprinted by permission of the publisher; from *Oxfam reports* (Winter 2002), reprinted by permission of Oxfam GB, 274 Banbury Road, Oxford OX2 7DZ; from *Red and White*, Bristol City FC programme, 1998; **Unit 2.5**: from *A Moveable Feast* by Ernest Hemingway (Jonathan Cape, 1964); from *Snowdonia* by H.L. Edlin (HMSO, 1963); **Unit 2.6**: from *The National Curriculum for English* (HMSO); from *Holland & Sherry News* (September 2001) on www.hollandandsherry.com; from www.news.bbc.co.uk – BBC News Online (7 April 2000), photograph of Bill Gates, reproduced by permission of Associated Press; **Unit 2.7**: from *The National Curriculum for English* (HMSO); from www.news.bbc.co.uk – BBC News Online (27 September 2001); from *The Whispering Land* by Gerald Durrell (Penguin Books, 1961); **Unit 2.8**: from www.lake-district.gov.uk; from *Denning: The Family Story* by Lord Denning (Hamlyn, 1982); from 'Why Do It To A Fish?' on People for the Ethical Treatment of Animals (PETA) website www.peta.org, reprinted by permission of PETA; **Unit 2.9**: from *Heroes* by John Pilger (Vintage, 2001), reprinted by permission of The Random House Group Ltd; **Unit 2.11**: from *The Times Magazine* (25 January 2003); from 'The 12.10 to Leeds' by Ian Jack from *Granta*, 73 (Spring 2001); **Unit 2.12**: from *Venice* by Jan Morris (Faber & Faber, 1960); **Unit 3.1**: from 'Families rely on Soaps to Trigger debate' by John Carvel in *The Guardian* (17 October 2002), © *The Guardian*, reprinted by permission of the publisher; **Unit 3.2**: from 'Doom And Boom' by Philip French in *The Observer* (16 February 2003), © *The Observer*, reprinted by permission of the publisher; from the 'Energy Review' on Friends of the Earth website www.foe.co.uk, reprinted by permission of Friends of the Earth; **Unit 3.3**: from 'Should Sven go part time?' by Gordon Strachan in *The Observer* (16 February 2003), © Gordon Strachan, reprinted by permission of the publisher; from Leader Column, No Byline in *The Observer* (16 February 2003), © *The Observer*, reprinted by permission of the publisher; from 'I don't keep up with the Zeta Jones' by David Aaronovitch in *The Observer* (16 February 2003), © *The Observer*, reprinted by permission of the publisher; **Unit 3.4**: from 'Comment' section of *The Independent* by Helen Storey (25 September 1999), reprinted by permission of the publisher; **Unit 3.5**: from *The Big Sleep* by Raymond Chandler (Penguin Books, 1948), copyright 1939 by Raymond Chandler, reprinted by permission of the publisher; from 'What a Waste' by Paul Brown in *The Guardian* (11 October 2000), © *The Guardian*, reprinted by permission of the publisher; **Unit 3.6**: views on Health and Mobile Phones from ARPANSA website www.arpansa.gov.au; **Unit 3.7**: from 'All teenagers to be forced to do community work' by Geraldine Hackett from *The Sunday Times* (1 July 2001), © Times Newspapers Limited, 2001, reprinted by permission of the publisher; **Unit 3.9**: 'Growing up on the front line; Life & Times' by Joan Simpson from *The Times* (10 April 1991), (© Times Newspapers Limited, 1991, reprinted by permission of the publisher; **Unit 3.10**: review of 'Da Ali G Show' by Mike Duffy from *Detroit Free Press* (1 February 2003) on www.freep.com; review of 'Da Ali G Show' by Lynn Elber, The Associated Press, in *The Cincinnati Enquirer* (21 February 2003) on www.enquirer.com; **Unit 3.12**: 'D'ya wanna be in my gang?' by Caroline Haydon from *The Independent* (31 October 2002), and letters in response, reprinted by permission of the publisher.

Every effort has been made to trace or contact all copyright holders. The publishers would be pleased to rectify any omissions brought to their notice at the earliest opportunity.

Illustrations by:
Linda Jeffrey, pages 7, 35/36, 50/52, 51, 54/57, 61, 80, 86, 87, 102, 118, 130, 146, 148
Carol Jonas, pages 20, 26/29, 38, 67, 72, 90, 98, 110, 122, 138
Ruth Palmer, pages 14, 23/24, 46, 58, 62, 94, 106, 114, 126, 134, 137, 144